Women Who Make the World Worse

Women Who Make the World Worse

and How Their Radical Feminist Assault Is Ruining Our Families, Military, Schools, and Sports

KATE O'BEIRNE

SENTINEL

SENTINEL
Published by the Penguin Group
Penguin Group (USA) Inc., 375 Hudson Street, New York, New York 10014, USA • Penguin
Group (Canada), 90 Eglinton Avenue East, Suite 700, Ontario, Canada M4P 2Y3 (a division of
Pearson Penguin Canada Inc.) • Penguin Books Ltd, 80 Strand, London WC2R 0RL, England •
Penguin Ireland, 25 St Stephen's Green, Dublin 2, Ireland (a division of Penguin Books Ltd) •
Penguin Group Australia Ltd, 250 Camberwell Road, Camberwell, Victoria 3124, Australia
(a division of Pearson Australia Group Pty Ltd) • Penguin Books India Pvt Ltd, 11 Community
Centre, Panchsheel Park, New Delhi – 110 017, India • Penguin Group (NZ), Cnr Airborne
and Rosedale Roads, Albany, Auckland 1310, New Zealand (a division of Pearson New Zealand
Ltd) • Penguin Books (South Africa) (Pty) Ltd, 24 Sturdee Avenue, Rosebank, Johannesburg 2196,
South Africa

Penguin Books Ltd, Registered Offices: 80 Strand, London WC2R 0RL, England

First published in 2006 by Sentinel, a member of Penguin Group (USA) Inc.

10   9   8   7   6   5   4   3   2   1

LIBRARY OF CONGRESS CATALOGING-IN-PUBLICATION DATA

O'Beirne, Kate.
    Women who make the world worse : and how their radical feminist assault is ruining our
    families, military, schools, and sports / Kate O'Beirne.
        p. cm.
    Includes index.
    ISBN 1-59523-009-2
    1. Feminism—United States—History. 2. Women's rights—United States—History.
    3. Women—United States—History. I. Title.
    HQ1426.O24 2005
    305.42'0973'09045—dc22   2005051715

Printed in the United States of America   •   Set in Weiss   •   Designed by Jaime Putorti

To my parents, Kay and Matt Walsh,
in gratitude for their gifts of faith, family,
. . . and all that jazz

Acknowledgments

Without the women in my life who make the world better, this book would not have been written. A different one may have been. I might have penned an angry screed condemning the patriarchal plot aimed at keeping women in our subservient place. But the women I am fortunate to know, who have shaped my life, don't believe such nonsense.

My wonderful sisters, Mary Ann, Virginia, and Rosemary, have shared the gift of our parents, whose selfless devotion and unfailing encouragement exemplified the kind of woman we hoped to become and the kind of man we hoped to marry. In turn, my sisters' love and encouragement have been gifts to me. To have sisters is to have best friends for life.

The other group of Sisters to whom I owe so much taught me from kindergarten through college. These Catholic nuns were women of character, compassion, and courage. They devoted their lives to the education of young women and provided a daily example of the feminine genius they fervently believed in and prayed we would come to prize. It was inconceivable to them that the young women in their charge weren't the equal of any man. They recognized that we had strengths to complement the masculine attributes of the boys in our brother school around the corner. But the nuns cautioned that we should be in no hurry to get the complementing under way. "The flower that blooms first dies first," we were frequently reminded.

My life has been enriched and any undertaking made easier by the encouragement of loyal friends. I know these generous women won't mind if I mention only one of them by name. I hope I have written a book that the late Barbara Olson would have loved. After Barbara was murdered on September 11, 2001, I knew we would somehow carry on without her, but I predicted it wouldn't be quite as much fun. I was right.

Along with millions of other women, I am indebted to the dedicated analysts and advocates who have no use for the destructive war between the sexes. Their rigorous research and commitment made this book possible. I want to thank Maggie Gallager, Barbara Dafoe Whitehead, Daphne de Marneffe, Suzanne Venker, Diana Furchtgott-Roth, Christine Stolba, Daphne Patai, Christina Hoff Sommers, Judith Kleinfeld, Jessica Gavora, Elaine Donnelly, Karlyn Bowman, Serrin Foster, and Erika Bachiochi.

But first there was Phyllis Schlafly. She recognized the threat posed by radical feminism when few did, and resolved to do something about it. But for her, the destructive feminist agenda would be enshrined in the Constitution. Taking on cultural liberalism is not for the faint of heart. Phyllis Schlafly's courage and fortitude are an inspiration.

I am grateful to *National Review.* I grew up enjoying an audio version of the magazine with my father reading his favorite bits aloud. He was one of William F. Buckley Jr.'s biggest fans even before his daughter was shown countless kindnesses by our legendary founding editor. Our publisher, Ed Capano, and president, Dusty Rhodes, unfailingly support their writers and editors. My accomplished colleagues Rich Lowry, Ramesh Ponnuru, Kathryn Jean Lopez, John Miller, Byron York, and Mike Potemra generously reviewed early manuscripts and helped me navigate the byways of book publishing. Given this collective talent, mistakes are obviously mine alone. In Washington, our cheerful and competent editorial associate, Liz Fisher, has masterfully juggled the demands of our multiple writers and authors.

My agent Lynn Chu's early enthusiasm for this book is much appreciated, and my editor, Bernadette Malone, was a constant source of ideas and encouragement.

Finally, I owe enormous thanks to the men in my life. My husband, Jim, and sons, Phil and John, are sorry representatives of the hostile patriarchy so alive in the imagination of the women who make the world worse. They are a constant source of love and support.

Contents

Introduction

On March 11, 2005, accused felon Brian Nichols overpowered Deputy Sheriff Cynthia Hall in the Atlanta courthouse where she worked, and killed four people before surrendering the following day. We weren't supposed to notice the insanity of a petite fifty-one-year-old grandmother guarding a former college football linebacker who had been caught with two sharpened door hinges in his socks earlier in the week. The local sheriff's office had adopted the politically correct premise that men and women are interchangeable and only misogynist males would deny a willing woman any job she sought. The four deaths in Atlanta are just a recent concrete example of what feminism has wrought.

I tried to warn you.

One spring day many years ago, the battle lines were drawn for a wholly new struggle that would have profound effects on our institutions and our politics. I found myself an early recruit in the looming struggle between the sexes.

The Equal Rights Amendment passed the United States Senate, 84–8, on March 22, 1972. One of the eight naysayers I proudly called my boss: Senator James L. Buckley of New York. At best, the sweeping social and legal effects of the amendment were unknown; at worst its deceptively simple language would impose a rigid sex sameness in every facet of American life. Fortunately, after an initial flurry of ratifications by a majority of the states, the amendment stalled short of the three quarters it needed. Today, the ERA is a relic, symbolically reintroduced every two years by aging feminists for old times' sake. A battle was won when the ERA was defeated, but feminists went on to win the war.

When I took up the case against the ERA, in discussions with law school classmates and in debates with NOW's founders, such as Karen DeCrow, my feminist opponents dismissed me as a weak-minded tool of the patriarchy. But if the fight was going to be about women's choices, I had freely made mine.

I strongly believed that women shouldn't face discrimination in employment or educational opportunities, and supported any necessary legislation to realize these worthy goals. I never believed that men and women were interchangeable, that women's equality rested on abortion rights, or that marriage and family life were a patriarchal plot to keep women in their submissive place. What I thought were pretty sensible, widely shared views were heretical to the ERA's staunch supporters. I learned early on that in the name of liberation the sisterhood meant to enforce a strict orthodoxy. Their tactics made me wonder how we were ever labeled the fairer sex.

Having been raised with three sisters and educated by women in a Catholic girls-only high school and college, it was jarring to suddenly find myself labeled as a traitor to my sex. Some of my best friends were women! It was a sure bet that my accusers weren't kidding. Humor was one of the first casualties in the battle between the sexes.

When the Bush administration lent its support to single-sex public schools, Eleanor Smeal protested, "You are doing girls no favor by putting them in all-girls schools." Women like Smeal, the former president of NOW, and current president of the Feminist Majority Foundation, regard my education as morally akin to apartheid. In truth, in high school and college we ran our own little female societies while the patriarchy was handed the bills. Isn't that an arrangement feminists long for? We girls were in charge of everything.

When self-pitying Anne Wilson Schaef echoes a familiar feminist lament by declaring, "To be born female in this culture means that you are born 'tainted,' that there is something intrinsically wrong with you that you can never change, that your birthright is one of innate inferiority," I think: she should have been on Knickerbocker Road in Manhasset, New York. In our conventional 1960s middle-class culture, we girls ran the neighborhood. We'd jump rope by the hour, with one end of the rope anchored to the bumper of a Rambler and some hapless little boy turning the other end until we released him from his duties.

At St. Mary's Girls' High School, which Eleanor Smeal believes didn't do me any favors, I was active in speech and debate and we regularly competed against both boys' and girls' teams. Sister Kateri, the nun who coached our team, trained us to go in for the kill. My parents wholly approved of the verbal combat. "You enjoy arguing; maybe you ought to be a lawyer," my father would suggest. No fan of lawyers ("they'll be the ruination of this country"), he may have wanted to see a lawyer he could love. It never occurred to him that the practice of law was unsuitable for a woman.

When I was a law student during the 1970s, women made up only 20 percent of my class and it took only a small verboten joke to provide evidence of my traitorous behavior. Law firms would come to campus to interview prospective associates, and we'd troop in for brief interviews with a recruiter. During one of these, the recruiter asked me, "What do you expect to be in ten years?" I was expected to say something about being a hardworking partner or about specializing in some esoteric area of the law or something equally dry. I said that I expected to be about five years older. This mildly amusing remark was met with an appreciative chuckle. Later that day, an angry female classmate came storming into the student lounge mumbling, "Where is she? I'll kill her." She had been asked the same question about her future plans and noticed that her questioner seemed distracted during her answer. When she finished her earnest recital, he laughingly told her that another classmate had responded, "Five years older." She immediately realized it must have been me. "You set us all back when you fool around like that," she fumed at me.

The incident revealed how the women's movement would operate. My friend was enforcing the monolith that holds that women all have to think and act alike. I was being told that we're not individuals to be judged separately but rather representatives of an oppressed class defined by a group identity. When feminists complain about the alleged glass ceiling, think about which of these two women students you'd rather work with. Someone who didn't take herself too seriously or a humorless, prickly pioneer dragging the weight of women's historical oppression around with her? Today, the world has been made worse because these humorless, prickly pioneers are winning.

The ERA's defeat was a hollow victory. In retrospect, what the feminists failed to achieve in that one fell, ill-considered legislative swoop was downright modest compared to their later success in reshaping every facet of American life. The evolution under way in women's roles was overtaken by a radical revolution that scored victories beyond feminists' wildest fantasies of thirty years ago. The changes they couldn't impose by constitutional amendment they have imposed through the schools, college faculties, and the culture, by judicial fiat and advocacy dressed up as legislation.

Don't be fooled by their contention that progress has been thwarted and there are miles to go before women achieve full equality. First, these women are chronically dissatisfied. And most radical feminists are qualified for only one job: professional feminist. Thousands of professional feminists can't declare victory and go home, because they would have no homes, they would have no jobs or prospects of jobs. They are generously paid, largely by taxpayers, but also by corporations anxious to look good on "women's issues," to be feminist theorists, academics, counselors, consultants, trainers, and advocates. They review textbooks and train teachers to erase those gruesome sex stereotypes, they conduct sexual harassment workshops for nervous corporations, they counsel cops and judges on domestic abuse, they "mainstream gender values" into college curriculums, and they advocate for women's rights at a network of feminist organizations.

Time and again, I would find myself as a minority voice on panels discussing "women's issues," and to my right and left would be professional feminists funded by my taxes. These women sit on review panels to give federal grants to each other, to study things only they care about. Every new federal law they design, aimed at addressing some inequality they identify, based on studies they've written, comes with hundreds of millions of dollars in feminist pork spending. The Violence Against Women Act is a striking example.

The gender warriors clearly benefited when their demonized enemy proved to have no stomach for the fight. The fearsome male patriarchy folded like a cheap Kate Spade knockoff. Men certainly weren't charmed into submission. The shrill feminists who made men the enemy took shrewd advantage of the fact that men hate arguing with women. They love their mothers, sisters, wives, and daughters. They want to please the women in their lives, and many men naively believed that giving feminists what they wanted would send them happily on their way.

Because radical feminists specialize in a moral intimidation that declares men guilty as a class, other women have to take on the women who make the world worse. In these pages you'll meet not only the women, fawned over by the media, who make the world worse but the truly courageous women who make the world better by defending our schools, families, military, and sports from the feminist assault.

The modern feminist movement has never enjoyed the allegiance of a majority of American women. Feminists regularly reassure one another by reporting that younger women readily identify themselves as feminists when they are asked whether they support the movement's "goals." The reassuring quiz used in speeches and classrooms typically asks: "Do you support equal pay for equal work? Do you think girls should be encouraged to study math and science? Do you think that women should be able to play sports if they want to? Should abortion be available to save women's lives?"

My own score is nearly perfect on this deceptive nonsense, and I am no feminist. There is little support for radical feminists' true aims. Questions honestly representing their agenda would include: "Do you think mothers who stay at home are betraying women's progress and hurting their children? Should standards be lowered so women can serve in physically demanding military jobs alongside men? If not enough women are playing sports, should men's teams be eliminated so athletes on campus are evenly split between the sexes? Should abortion be permitted on the eve of delivery?"

Flying under the false flag of "equal pay for equal work" and fueled by their persecution fantasies, modern feminists have been successfully advancing an agenda that demands radical social engineering to eliminate any differences between the sexes. They insist that any sex differences are the result of social construction—not biology—so they will deconstruct society. So little boys hop on the school bus each morning to head to reeducation classes where their pathology will be treated.

Feminists argue there are no innate sex differences—except where there are. Their orthodoxy holds that there are no sex differences when it comes to academic interest and abilities, or commitment to a professional career, or interest in playing sports, or fitness for combat duty. Got it? But wait: There are crucial sex differences when it suits feminists to recognize them: sensitivity to sexual banter, political behavior, women's "way of knowing," or their obvious general superiority. For example, according to Stephanie Davis, the executive director of Atlanta's Women's Foundation: "The feminism I think of is the one that embodies inclusivity, multiculturalism and the ability to change the world through the humanity that women do bring. I think if there were women in power in representative numbers—52 percent—I think that the World Trade Center would still be standing." (Note: whenever a feminist asserts the need for more women in power, read "liberal women." They do not mean Margaret Thatcher or Condoleezza Rice, or any woman who doesn't subscribe to their ideology.)

They talk "freedom and choice," but feminists are too contemptuous of dissenting women to allow them to choose freely how to live their lives without ridicule and disdain.

The modern women's movement is totalitarian in its methods, radical in its aims, and dishonest in its advocacy. Coercion is employed through the courts to enforce its unpopular agenda, on issues like abortion and gender quotas. Radical feminists warn of the perilous gender gap threatening any politician who doesn't knuckle under to their demands, but rarely seem able to win elections. They confidently predicted the defeats of Ronald Reagan and George W. Bush at the hands of angry women.

American women have more freedom in their personal and professional lives than any man or woman has ever enjoyed in recorded history. The unprecedented opportunities we enjoy come with tough choices and trade-offs. Millions of women have learned they can have it all—fulfilling careers and families—but not at the same time unless they are willing to feel torn and conflicted. Many others make a different trade-off and try to sequence education, work, and children. I was either home full-time or doing shift duty with my husband until both my sons were in school full-time. These trade-offs families freely make to balance their lives go a long way toward explaining the phony "wage gap" that feminists politicize as evidence of persistent sex discrimination.

With women making up 60 percent of all college graduates, you might think it would be tough for feminists to argue that our universities are plagued by pervasive sex discrimination. You'd be wrong. The National Women's Law Center sees "enduring sex discrimination" because 96 percent of students in cosmetology classes are female, while male students make up 93 percent of future welders and carpenters. In the name of seeking equal opportunity, gender warriors demand legally enforced equal outcomes. Before they succeed in enforcing strict gender quotas in the classroom, as they have in college sports, they have to be stopped.

Feminism's most destructive effects sometimes masquerade as well-intentioned benevolence. New York City announced in 2003 that a free breakfast would be provided to *all* 1.1 million children in its schools, regardless of family income. This sounds charitable and even-handed. But lurking behind this government substitution for the traditional responsibilities of families is the feminist insistence that parents be unburdened of the demands of their children. Let

Hillary Clinton's village worry about seeing that children have some-thing to eat in the morning. What sorry excuse for a parent is unable to rustle up a bowl of cereal and a piece of toast for a child heading off to school?

Many of the welcome changes in women's prospects that femi-nists take credit for were well under way when Betty Friedan was a frustrated housewife seething in the suburbs. In 1963, nearly half of American women worked outside the home, pursuing opportunities all by their helpless selves. For the dedicated nuns who taught us in the 1960s, it was unthinkable that we wouldn't go to college and prepare for a career. My own suburban mother was happy, fulfilled, and determined that her four daughters have advantages she didn't—just as generations of mothers before her hoped for the same for their sons and daughters.

But long before NOW held its first organizational meeting, there were female role models who exemplified initiative, intelli-gence, and independence. America's first large network of profes-sional women was Catholic nuns. In the 1900s, they built and ran the country's largest private school and hospital systems. These women were nurses, teachers—and CEOs.

In their ignorance and arrogance feminists view the Catholic Church in particular as little more than a shrine to the male patri-archy, ignoring the historic role of Christianity in elevating the sta-tus of women, beginning in ancient Rome. The Catholic Church recognizes women from the fourteenth and sixteenth centuries as Doctors of the Church, honored for their brilliant scholarship. Mis-sionary nuns who traveled the globe to open schools for girls in in-hospitable cultures dismissive of female education have done more for the well-being of the world's women than all the gender warriors in the world. The sacrificial selflessness that inspired these women's extraordinary accomplishments offends feminist sensibilities.

The positive legacy of the modern women's movement is dubious or trivial. Assigning male names to hurricanes and putting changing tables in men's rooms come to mind. The negative legacy has been devastating. Radical feminist premises have achieved the status of revealed truths in our schools, in the military, in the halls of Congress, and where we work and worship. Our institutions are weaker, our culture feminized, yet coarser, and the burdens of government are greater.

In her landmark book, Friedan argued that mothers had to get the heck out of the house because their children were being harmed by their "over-nurturing." Today, studies find that parents spend 50 percent less time with their children than they did forty years ago, primarily because so many mothers work outside the home. By every available measurement, including school achievement and the incidence of delinquency, depression, sexual promiscuity, suicide, and substance abuse, the well-being of American children has declined in recent decades. Nice work, Betty, the over-nurturing of children problem has been licked!

The sexual revolution feminists champion has been a disaster. In popular women's studies textbooks, girls are encouraged to believe sex is as meaningless as they assume it is to young men. Now, thirty-year-old men can enjoy a perpetual adolescence of sex without consequences or commitment, and women despair of ever finding a marriageable mate. "Bring back the date" is the plaintive appeal of college women who prefer romance and intimacy over the current campus regime of "hooking up."

When traditional manners and mores were scorned as a product of a patriarchy bent on keeping women in their place, laws and litigation were substituted in a destructive attempt to govern relations between the sexes. Male chivalry protected women far better than feminist lawsuits over girlie calendars and dirty jokes.

Legal protections women used to enjoy, in divorce and child custody for example, had to be banished as a matter of equal rights according to feminist legal theorists, one of whom unfortunately now sits on the Supreme Court. Justice Ruth Bader Ginsburg explains, "Differential treatment on the basis of sex was rationalized with a kind of romantic paternalism, which didn't put women on a pedestal, but in a cage." During her theorist years, in her vigilance to see the elimination of any and all sex differences in the law and culture, Justice Ginsburg proposed replacing Mother's Day and Father's Day with Parents' Day, supported coed prisons, and believed the Girl Scouts and Boy Scouts dangerously perpetuated debilitating stereotypes. No different treatment under the law escaped her notice, however benign. One of the cases she argued before the Supreme Court as a feminist advocate in 1976 struck down an Oklahoma law that allowed women to purchase beer at age eighteen but required men to wait until they were twenty-one. How about a toast to such a crusading gender warrior?

Justice Ginsburg takes great pride in her personal dedication "to place women's rights permanently on the human rights agenda." The old inspirational rallying cry for "Equal Rights, Now" is tough to square with the most common call of campus feminists today: "Vagina, vagina," they chant in an exercise of alleged "empowerment" during performances of *The Vagina Monologues*, one of modern culture's particularly vulgar offerings.

Inspired by Eve Ensler's viciously antimale play, on more than five hundred campuses Valentine's Day has been replaced by V-Day (short for Vagina Day). Hollywood heavies, including Susan Sarandon, Melanie Griffith, and Glenn Close, have eagerly sought roles in the obscene performance and younger women now decorate their campuses with flyers declaring, "My Vagina Is Flirty," or, "My Vagina Is Huggable." We've come a long way, baby. This is what the noble effort to win the franchise and the right to own property has been reduced to.

Jane Fonda swooned after she performed in the play. She called the gig "one of the most memorable and empowering experiences of my life." Gloria Steinem explains that it's only right that the vagina replace the heart as a symbol of Valentine's Day because "the shape we call a heart resembles the vulva far more than the organ that shares its name." The vulva "was [you guessed it] reduced from power to romance by centuries of male dominance."

The former Barbarella apparently believes that it's real progress to go from being a sex object to a sex organ. In Jane Fonda's autobiography we learned that the men in her life never failed to fail her. Her father, Henry, was distant and cold; her first husband, film director Roger Vadim, demanded group sex with Jane and women she recruited to please him. Her second husband, the antiwar activist Tom Hayden, announced on Fonda's fifty-first birthday that he was in love with another woman; and she caught her third husband, media mogul Ted Turner, cheating on her within a month of their wedding.

The feminist slogan "the personal is political" means that the ideology of the modern women's movement was shaped by the personal experiences of its founders—and they weren't pretty. Betty Friedan's mother had "a complete inability to nurture" and reportedly made her feel unwanted and ugly. Friedan went into psychoanalysis as an adult to address her rage at her mother. In her autobiography, she claimed her marriage was abusive. Australian feminist Germaine Greer, author of *The Female Eunuch*, described her childhood as filled with pain and humiliation, with an abusive mother and a father she later said she never really knew. She has written, "If I put my arms around him, he would grimace and pretend to shudder and put me from him."

Gloria Steinem's father abandoned the family, and she was left as a young girl to care for her mentally ill mother. These are the women whose views on men and marriage inform the women's movement. Gloria Steinem's dysfunctional childhood persuaded her that "you become a non-person when you get married" and "a woman needs a man like a fish needs a bicycle." Thousands of her acolytes adopted the defiant slogan born of misery and abandonment.

In 2000, at age sixty-six, the never-married Steinem wed an anti-apartheid activist in a Cherokee ceremony.

The destructive work of the women who make the world worse is not done, not by a long shot. During a 1999 White House ceremony in celebration of National Women's History Month, First Lady Hillary Clinton recalled past struggles "as we move into the next century and the next stage of our journey toward full participation in public life . . ."

We know where Hillary Clinton hopes her own journey will take her. You've been warned.

Women Who

Make the

World Worse

I | How Radical Feminists Have Weakened the Family

The traditional family boosts the health, happiness, and wealth of husbands, wives, and children and raises the blood pressure of a certain kind of woman. Betty Friedan's 1963 *The Feminine Mystique* is typically included on lists of the one hundred most influential books of the last century. In a chapter entitled "The Comfortable Concentration Camp," she likened the passivity and hopelessness of American POWs in Korea to American women trapped at home with children in the suburbs. She later wrote, "For fear of being alone, I almost lost my own self-respect trying to hold on to a marriage that was based no longer on love but on dependent hate. It was easier for me to start the women's movement which was needed to change society than to change my own personal life."[1]

Friedan got a divorce in 1969, but unfortunately not before she expounded on the merits of Marxist economics, persuaded far too many women that a selfless devotion to their families was a recipe for misery, helped to create the National Organization for Women (NOW), and destructively politicized relations between the sexes. Over the next decades, Friedan's fans moved beyond her criticisms of mothers at home and launched a hostile assault on marriage and family life.

The radical demand for androgyny and personal autonomy is irreconcilable with the need for different sex roles and mutual self-sacrifice between parents raising their offspring. Influential feminists see two major problems with the family that inhibit women's equality—husbands and fathers. Their advocacy and propaganda have eroded support for the family as an indispensable institution for both individuals and society.

MARRIAGE UNDER ASSAULT

In 1969, Marlene Dixon, a sociology professor at the University of Chicago, wrote, "The institution of marriage is the chief vehicle for the perpetuation of the oppression of women; it is through the role of wife that the subjugation of women is maintained. In a very real way the role of wife has been the genesis of women's rebellion throughout history."[2]

That same year, Kate Millett's *Sexual Politics* was published. What began as a thesis for the Columbia University doctoral candidate became a celebrated call for the end of a patriarchal institution that treated women like chattel. In 1970, Robin Morgan, a founder of *Ms.* magazine, was calling marriage "a slavery-like practice," and arguing, "We can't destroy the inequities between men and women until we destroy marriage."[3] The following year, Australian feminist Germaine Greer's *The Female Eunuch* argued that married women had to save themselves by fleeing from their marriages in favor of "rambling organic structures."[4]

By 1972, the angry screeds against marriage were being dressed up with academic adornments. In her influential book *The Future of Marriage*, Pennsylvania State University sociologist Jessie Bernard claimed that the "destructive nature" of marriage harmed women's mental and emotional health. In short, according to Bernard, "Being a housewife makes women sick."[5] The fact that married women regularly reported that they were happier than unmarried women was dismissed as a symptom of this marital illness. "To be happy in a relationship which imposes so many impediments on her, as traditional marriage does, women must be slightly mentally ill." It was their oppression speaking when wives reported satisfaction with their lives. "Women accustomed to expressing themselves freely could not be happy in such a relationship."[6]

Although the late Professor Bernard's pronouncements were those of a left-wing ideologue with a radical agenda, she was considered one of the top women sociologists in the world, and according to *The Boston Globe*, her twenty-three books established her as "the preeminent scholar of the women's movement." She held visiting professorships at Princeton and at the University of California. In *The Future of Motherhood* she argued that being a mother was also hazardous to women's health. She saw the desire for children as a sexist social construction and believed that many women preferred celibacy to "the degradation of most male-female sexual relationships." Professor Bernard sounded a warning about what truly liberated women could expect: "Men will resist and punish them; unliberated women, brainwashed not only to accept their slavery in marriage but also to love it, will resist them."[7] The Center for Women's Policy Studies established a Jessie Bernard Wise Women award to recognize similar worthy insights.

Many establishment figures share Bernard's views. Laura Singer, who was president of the American Association for Marriage and Family Therapy in the 1970s, has explained, "I wouldn't say that marriage and self-actualization are *necessarily* mutually exclusive, but they are difficult to achieve together."[8]

If these attacks on marriage strike you as extreme, you have some surprising company. Twenty years after she helped launch the modern women's movement, even Betty Friedan was criticizing her feminist sisters for their hostility to family life. In her 1981 book *The Second Stage,* she wrote: "The women's movement is being blamed, above all, for the destruction of the family." She cited the increase in divorces, in single-parent households, and in the number of women living alone and asked, "Can we keep on shrugging all this off as enemy propaganda—'their problem, not ours'? I think we must at least admit and begin openly to discuss feminist denial of the importance of family, of women's own needs to give and get love and nurture, tender loving care."[9]

This time Betty Friedan's appeals fell on deaf feminist ears. The scholarship and sentiment that sounded dire warnings about marriage's harmful effects on women's well-being and ambitions had found an enthusiastic audience in women's studies programs and was popularized by journalists like Barbara Ehrenreich, a former columnist for *Time* magazine.

Writing from that powerful perch, Ehrenreich repeatedly denigrated marriage and family life. She advocated that the government concentrate on promoting "good divorces" rather than attempt to strengthen marriages and argued that the only problem with single-parent households was the lack of sufficient government support. She used the Menendez brothers and O. J. Simpson cases as an opportunity to share her opinion about the malevolent forces afoot in American families. The murders should prompt us to think "that the family may not be the ideal and perfect living arrangement after all—that it can be a nest of pathology and a cradle of gruesome violence." She asserted that "millions flock to therapy groups" and "we are all, it is often said, 'in recovery.' And from what? Our families, in most cases." She cited the "long and honorable tradition of 'anti-family' thought" and quoted Edmund Leach, the renowned British anthropologist, stating that "far from being the basis of a good society, the family, with its narrow privacy and tawdry secrets, is the source of all discontents."[10]

Marlo Thomas and her pals, including Lily Tomlin, Bea Arthur, and Whoopi Goldberg, literally sang the praises of never-formed or broken families. Thomas's earlier *Free to Be . . . You and Me* attempted to overcome nasty sex stereotypes and create a more welcoming world for boys who played with dolls. In her *Free to Be . . . a Family*, any arrangement at all was promoted as just fine for raising children. The book and album wanted to teach children that "if the people whom you live with are happy to see your face, that's a family." The stories, songs and poems were "really about the family as it exists today, not the family as a storybook idea."[11]

During the 2004 campaign, Teresa Heinz Kerry reflected a casual contempt for the role of wife and mother when she proclaimed that Laura Bush hadn't worked at a "real job . . . since she's been grown up." Laura Bush worked as a teacher and librarian for ten years, before giving up her career in education to raise her twin daughters. Most people, who haven't inherited a condiments empire and the resources to allow them to keep busy handing out fat foundation grants, think being a wife and mother is a "real job" for a "grown-up."

Before long, the antipathy to marriage infected the academy and was reflected in social science textbooks. When a nonpartisan group studied twenty textbooks used in eight thousand college courses in the mid-nineties, they found, "These books repeatedly suggest that marriage is more a problem than a solution. The potential costs of marriage to adults, particularly women, often receive exaggerated treatment, while the benefits of marriage, both to individuals and society, are frequently downplayed or ignored."[12]

In *Changing Families*, Judy Root Aulette, a sociology professor at the University of North Carolina at Charlotte, didn't mention a single beneficial effect of marriage in the three chapters she devoted to the subject (one of which was titled "Battering and Marital Rape").[13] She did find room to approvingly cite Friedrich Engels stating that marriage was "created for a particular purpose: to control women and children."[14]

While Professor Aulette had a lot to learn about the institution of marriage, she was well schooled in the politics of phony grievances. She accused the report's author of trying "to get rid of my voice, and my right to be in a classroom and present a feminist point of view."[15]

In her textbook, Maxine Baca Zinn proved herself worthy of a Jessie Bernard Wise Women award when she wrote, "If marriage is so difficult for wives, why do the majority surveyed judge themselves as happy? . . . [The reason] is that happiness is interpreted by wives in terms of conformity. Since they are conforming to society's expectations, this must be happiness."[16]

The study's author, Professor Norval Glenn of the University of Texas, explained that the textbooks studied represented "the distilled essence of the current conventional wisdom" and were used to train the next generation of counselors, social workers, therapists, and teachers. He illustrated the conventional wisdom by contrasting the number of pages in each book focusing on the benefits of marriage for adults—less than one—with the pages per book devoted to domestic violence—twelve.[17]

MARRIAGE BENEFITS MEN AND WOMEN

Professor Linda Waite of the University of Chicago filled a well-researched book with the good news about marriage. In *The Case for Marriage: Why Married People Are Happier, Healthier, and Better Off Finan-*

cially, Waite, a self-described liberal Democrat, and her conservative co-author, Maggie Gallagher, detailed the research findings that thoroughly refute Jessie Bernard and her acolytes' case against marriage. Linda Waite saw the notion that marriage was a much better deal for men than women as "the most powerful and persuasive" of the modern myths about marriage. She thought it was important for young women to be well-informed before they make their choices. "If we pretend that women are not advantaged by being married, we are doing them a great disservice."

Among Waite and Gallagher's findings: Because wives influence husbands to take better care of themselves, men do get more health benefits from marriage than women, but both married men and women express "very high and very similar levels of satisfaction with their marriages" and are similarly committed to their spouses. Women gain more financially from marriage than men do, and while both sexes are winners in sexual satisfaction, women gain even more owing to the sense of commitment that improves their sex life. And, when a wide range of disorders is considered, both sexes enjoy a boost in mental health.[18] In fact, married women are generally less depressed than *Sex and the City*'s Carrie Bradshaw and her single sisters.[19]

A well-respected study found that similar percentages of married women and men (41 percent and 38 percent) report they are "very happy," rates that are far higher than for those who have never married or are divorced. Social psychologist David G. Myers, author of *The Pursuit of Happiness*, strongly endorses Waite and Gallagher's conclusions. "The idea that women are happier if they are unmarried and men happier if they are married is blatantly untrue. The evidence is mountainous in the other direction."[20]

Unlike other liberal women engaged in research on family issues, Dr. Waite had no preconceived notions or ideological axes to grind when she began to look at the data on marital status and mortality ten years ago. She was aware of other researchers looking at earnings data and health issues, but no one had put together the big picture. Waite recognized, "There's a general pattern here that nobody's noticed. All of the big things in life—good outcomes for children, health, long life—depend on marriage." This insight became the subject of a speech she delivered to the Population Association of America as its president in 1995.[21]

DIVORCE HURTS

Professor Waite and her colleagues have more recently published a study on divorce that showed that unhappily married people were no happier after their marriages ended. They analyzed data from a national survey on families and households and found, "When the adults who said they were unhappily married in the late 1980s were interviewed again five years later, those who had divorced were on average still unhappy or even less happy, while those who stayed in their marriages on average had moved past the bad times and were at a happier stage."[22]

Waite, who has been married for over thirty years, has a married daughter and a daughter with cerebral palsy who lives at home. She was married as an undergraduate and divorced from her first husband after four years with no children. She explains that her case against divorce is less applicable to the kind of short, early union she had. "It's very different. You're not leaving somebody who's financially dependent, you haven't built years of friendships, you don't have kids, you're not as much a working single unit as people who are married for a long time."[23]

Waite explains that once children are present, the case against divorce becomes stronger. Professor Waite and Maggie Gallagher looked at the effect of divorce on children in their book and concluded that children were usually not better off when their parents split up. They pointed out that divorce might end marital conflict for parents, but it doesn't end "what really bothers kids: parental conflict." Their research indicates, "Children of divorce also have less money, live in poorer neighborhoods, go to poorer schools, and do worse in school than children of married parents—even if those marriages have a high degree of conflict."[24]

In their book *Generation at Risk*, two liberal social scientists estimated that only about a third of divorces with children involved are so troubled that children are likely to benefit from the break-up. The remaining 70 percent of divorces involve low-conflict marriages where children are less harmed than they would be if their parents separated.[25]

FRACTURED FAMILIES AND DISPOSABLE DADS

In the past, the majority of Americans believed that unhappily married couples should stay together for the sake of their children. Now, only 15 percent agree that "when there are children in the family, parents should stay together even if they don't get along."[26] When the traditional virtues of self-sacrifice and duty lose in a conflict with the feminist doctrine of self-fulfillment and personal autonomy, children pay a very steep price.

In an ominous sign that the well-being of children is unlikely to take precedence over the desires of adults any time soon, among young people there is little appreciation for the benefits of marriage and widespread support for "alternative lifestyles" as perfectly suitable for raising children. A national survey of high school seniors found that although a large majority of these teenagers expect to marry, less than a third of girls and only slightly more than a third of boys believe "that most people will have fuller and happier lives if they choose legal marriage rather than staying single or just living with someone." More than half of both boys and girls think out-of-wedlock childbearing is a "worthwhile lifestyle."[27]

In 1988, among never-married people between the ages of eighteen and thirty-four, 64 percent of males and 56 percent of females thought "those who want children should get married." In 2002, only 51 percent of males and 42 percent of females in this age group thought having children and being married shouldn't be separate pursuits.[28]

While the pathetic plight of wives and mothers was being peddled by women like Bernard, Aulette, and Zinn, others were making the case that dads are dispensable.

Male lions roar to protect their young from threatening predators, penguin pops balance fragile eggs on their feet in frigid temperatures, while adult male elephants temper the delinquent behavior of the young bulls. When the National Fatherhood Initiative used these arresting thirty-second images from the animal kingdom to depict the importance of fathers in their "Nature of Fatherhood" ad campaign, they drove some feminists wild. NOW raised an alarm about the "dangerous policy" of paternal responsibility being promoted by the initiative, which hoped to encourage fathers to commit to marriage and parenting.

An article that argued "neither mothers nor fathers are unique or essential" was promoted to bolster the case that "NOW Knows Best." In "Deconstructing the Essential Father," published in the influential *American Psychologist* in 1999, the authors maintained that children are perfectly fine as long as they have "parenting figures" of either sex, who need not be biologically related. Predictably, the authors favored policies that support the legitimacy of "diverse family structures" rather than "privileging the two-parent, heterosexual, married family." Fatherhood is a retrograde gender role and therefore verboten.

The academics did not just dismiss the unique contributions of fathers as unimportant. It was argued that a father's presence in the home extracts an overlooked cost because "some fathers' consumption of family resources in terms of gambling, purchasing alcohol, cigarettes, or other nonessential commodities, actually increases women's workload and stress level." So, message to moms: Throw the bums out.

Professor Louise B. Silverstein, a Yeshiva University psychology professor and family therapist, co-authored the study that sought "to create an ideology that defines the father-child bond as independent of the father-mother relationship."[29] Professor Silverstein is a past president of the American Psychological Association's Division of Family Psychology and chairman (a title that could put her in therapy) of the Feminist Family Therapy Task Force within the APA Division of the Psychology of Women. Her 1999 article making the case for throwaway dads won the Association for Women in Psychology's Distinguished Publication Award.

From the indispensable Maggie Gallagher it won condemnation. Gallagher graduated from Yale University in 1982. Married with two sons, this Portland, Oregon, native lives in New York and is a syndicated columnist and president of the Institute for Marriage and Public Policy. The author of three books, she has been an editor of *National Review* and a senior editor of the Manhattan Institute's *City Journal.* George Gilder called her first book, *Enemies of Eros: How the Sexual Revolution Is Killing Family, Marriage, and Sex, and What We Can Do About It,* published in 1989, "the best book ever written on men, women and marriage."

Maggie Gallagher has mastered the social science research on marriage, the family, and child well-being to become a leading authority on the most personal public-policy questions we face. She devotes her formidable skills to debunking clichés and conventional wisdom about love, marriage, and children and has the fortitude to challenge a culture more interested in self-gratification to confront the consequences of our failure to keep our commitments.

After having some fun with Dr. Silverstein's conclusion that "both men and women have the same biological potential for nurturing" based on her examination of the behavior of marmoset fathers, Gallagher deconstructs Silverstein's deconstruction handiwork. "Our new desire to strengthen marriage is in their view just a scary attempt to reassert 'the cultural hegemony of traditional values, such as heterocentrism, Judeo-Christian marriage, and male power and privilege.' It leads to horrible, unrealistic policies—like giving job help to low-income married fathers (and not just welfare mothers), or a more marriage-friendly tax code. Instead, these hard-headed professors urge more practical solutions, like reconstructing traditional masculine ideology so men care for infants as much as women."

Maggie Gallagher incisively confronts the fundamental questions that Silverstein ignores. "Under what conditions are children likely to fare best? And, are adults obligated to provide, if they can, the best situation for their kids?"[30] Answers: Living with their married biological parents, and Yes.

Louise Silverstein is the glorified guru of gender warriors, but Cornell University professor Urie Bronfenbrenner, who was widely regarded as one of the world's leading scholars in developmental psychology, child-rearing, and human ecology—the interdisciplinary field he created—strongly disagreed with her Dispensable Dad thesis. "Controlling for factors such as low income, children growing up in father-absent households are at a greater risk for experiencing a variety of behavioral and educational problems, including extremes of hyperactivity and withdrawal; lack of attentiveness in the classroom; difficulty in deferring gratification; impaired academic achievement; school misbehavior; absenteeism; dropping out; involvement in socially alienated peer groups; and the so-called 'teen-age syndrome' of behaviors that tend to hang together—smoking, drinking, early and frequent sexual experience, and in the more extreme cases, drugs, suicide, vandalism, violence and criminal acts."[31]

In his defense of responsible fatherhood, Karl Zinsmeister counters Marlo Thomas's dismissal of the traditional family as a "storybook idea" by reminding us of its indispensability for men, women, and children. "It's when a culture stops upholding the paternal rituals, rules, and rewards that fathering withers. . . . Some people have actually convinced themselves families can do fine without fathers. They're wrong. Wherever men are not lured or corralled into concerning themselves with their children and mates, decent human society fades . . . the magic ingredients needed to tie men to their children are the ancient ones: Sexual restraint and enduring marriage."[32] When men are committed to protecting and providing for their families, wives and children benefit and so too do husbands.

Studies show that men become more economically productive after they marry, with married men earning between 10 and 40 percent more than single men with similar education and job experience. Marriage also increases median family income, which more than doubled between 1947 and 1977. Over the past twenty years, the growth in median family income has slowed, increasing by just 9.6 percent, in large part because married couples, who do better economically, make up a decreasing proportion of all families.[33]

In Britain, 49 percent of all births are illegitimate. In a sign that the British public has had its fill with the social and financial costs of unwed childbearing, three unmarried sisters and their babies recently made front-page news. MUM AT 12, MUM AT 16, MUM AT 14, the headlines blared. The father of the sixteen-year-old's baby is a thirty-eight-year-old man in a "long-term relationship" with her; he lives with his parents. Their divorced mother had been married twice, but never to the fathers of her daughters. She became a grandmother three times in a year.

While most of the commentary criticized the intergenerational illegitimacy and complained that taxpayers had to pick up the considerable tab, Germaine Greer surfaced to celebrate the self-actualization of young girls doing their own thing. "Social historians will tell you that illegitimacy is highly hereditary. There have always been women like Yeats' Crazy Jane whose gardens grow 'nothing but babies and washing.' They live in an alternative society that is matrilineal, matrifocal, and matrilocal, a society that the patriarchy has always feared and hated."[34] The "alternative society" Greer celebrates is on the brink of representing a majority of British births.

In 1960, only 9 percent of all children lived in single-parent households. Presently in the United States, almost one third of children are born to single mothers. A larger number of children will see their parents divorced before their eighteenth birthday. Two thirds of black children are born out of wedlock. Over half of American children will spend all or part of their childhood without their father in the home.

According to my former colleague, the Heritage Foundation's poverty guru Robert Rector, "The collapse of marriage is the principal cause of child poverty and a host of other social ills. A child raised by a never-married mother is seven times more likely to live in poverty than a child raised by his biological parents in an intact marriage." Nearly two thirds of poor children live in single-parent homes, and an additional 1.3 million children are born out of wedlock every year.[35] We have never experienced so many children growing up without knowing what it means to live with the daily support and attention of their fathers.

Half of children living without their fathers have never been in their father's home, and one study found that only 27 percent of children over age four saw their father at least once a week, while 31 percent had no contact at all in the previous year.[36]

In *The Abolition of Marriage*,[37] Maggie Gallagher reminds us, "When we tell our girls that becoming a single mother—through divorce or failure to marry—is a perfectly acceptable lifestyle choice, we forget that our boys are listening too. And this is what they hear: Men aren't necessary. Women can do it alone. Women and children are usually better off without men. Breadwinning oppresses women and children. Marriage and breadwinning can be hard. Why do it, if you are only oppressing the ones you love?"

Barbara Dafoe Whitehead is co-director of the National Marriage Project at Rutgers University. She famously concluded in an *Atlantic Monthly* article that "Dan Quayle Was Right" following the feminist fits over the vice president's *Murphy Brown* comments. Dr. Whitehead recently reported, "According to some researchers, growing up with both married parents in a low-conflict marriage is so important to child well-being that it is replacing race, class, and neighborhood as the greatest source of difference in child outcomes."[38]

According to the National Marriage Project, men today are increasingly staying single longer, fathering more illegitimate children, cohabiting rather than marrying, and divorcing in larger numbers. In 1970, only 7 percent of men between the ages thirty-five and forty-four had never married, compared with 18 percent today.

The National Fatherhood Initiative that NOW's feminists rail against as a patriarchal plot offers some inescapable "Father Facts." The rate of child abuse in single-parent households is nearly twice the rate of child abuse in two-parent families. Even after controlling for factors like family background and neighborhood variables, boys who grew up outside of intact marriages were, on average, more than twice as likely to end up in jail as other boys, and twice as likely to use illegal drugs.

Intact families are a far more effective "program" than are most government schemes to reduce poverty, child abuse, crime, and drug abuse, or to boost educational outcomes.

Although costly to men, women, children, and taxpayers, opposition to the traditional family is growing. The influential American Law Institute (ALI) recently released a report arguing that family law should be reformed so that marriage and cohabitation are treated equally and that marriage should be redefined as a gender-neutral arrangement in order to accommodate same-sex couples. These lawyers want to wipe out biology as a basis for parenthood in order to ensure "family diversity."

Professor Katharine Bartlett, a feminist scholar and dean of Duke University's law school, is one of the principal authors of the ALI report. She explains that her passion is "the value I place on family diversity and on the freedom of individuals to choose from a variety of family forms. This same value leads me to be generally opposed to efforts to standardize families into a certain type of nuclear family because a majority may believe this is the best kind of family or because it is the most deeply rooted ideologically in our traditions." Ignoring the overwhelming evidence about the benefits to family members and society from traditional marriage, Professor Bartlett attributes its support to either ignorant belief or blind ideology, befitting her status as a celebrated feminist scholar.[39]

VIOLENCE AGAINST THE TRUTH, AND THE TAXPAYER

In 1994, women who longed to see marriage regarded as an inherently abusive relationship and all men as potential assailants won a huge victory with passage of the Violence Against Women Act (VAWA). In that classic Washington game, a member of Congress who dared to oppose a measure with such a loaded title would be cast as probably favoring or, at best, condoning violence against women. Antimale activism won another federal imprimatur. One can recognize that physical abuse within a relationship should never be viewed as a "private matter" and not support enacting an ideological agenda dressed up as legislation.

The new federal law came with $1.6 billion to address what its proponents insisted was a national epidemic. Physical assault is a crime in all fifty states, but VAWA elevated violence against women above other crimes based on the sex of the victim. The law created a permanent lobby to hype the problem and a huge jobs program for feminist activists. Once the law was in place, Attorney General Janet Reno and Health and Human Services secretary Donna Shalala got right to work and issued a "Community Checklist" of important steps to take to protect women.

The National Advisory Council on Violence Against Women sees to it that communities are continually harangued to get with the program. Churches are told they should sponsor educational seminars for their congregations (jobs for feminists!), get training in how to understand domestic violence (more jobs), and include information about domestic violence in all their marriage preparation classes (given the high risk that violence will be in the happy couple's future). Colleges and universities should train students, faculty, and staff (more jobs) on how to recognize signs of abuse and target special audiences, like athletes (men obviously prone to violence), for specialized training (additional jobs).

Law enforcement is told that domestic violence "must be treated with the highest priority, regardless of the severity of the offense charged or injuries inflicted." Here too there is a need for "ongoing multidisciplinary domestic violence and sexual assault training for police, prosecutors, judges, advocates, defenders, service providers, child protection workers, educators and others." Lots and lots of jobs here. Health care professionals are told to incorporate training on domestic violence in all health education curricula (jobs) and arrange for presentations on domestic violence at annual, regional, and local meetings (jobs).

All workplaces are told that they should set up training programs for all their supervisors and managers so they can learn how to respond to employee victims of domestic violence (jobs again).

To reach the obvious perpetrators of all this domestic abuse of women, the sports community is advised to run public service announcements during broadcasts of sporting events.

The federal National Advisory Council helpfully provides information so women can determine whether they've been the victims of domestic abuse. According to the Department of Health and Human Services, "There are clear signs to help you know if you are being abused. If the person you love or live with does any of these things to you, it's time to get help: [the list includes] monitors what you're doing all the time, criticizes you for little things, controls how you spend your money, humiliates you in front of others." The serious abuse some women suffer has to be trivialized in order to create enough "abuse" to justify all the services, training, and advocacy feminists are now paid to provide.

In order to reach presumptive future abusers, the federal government also publishes a series of brochures called *Coaching Boys into Men* aimed at adult men for the benefit of boys in their lives who are inherently at risk of being abusive. They are told that boys hear "all kinds of messages about what it means to 'be a man'—that they have to be tough and in control." The pamphlets explain, "Boys need your advice on how to behave toward girls," and "If you see or hear things that depict violence against women, tell him what you think about it." (There is apparently no coordination between a Pentagon bent on putting women in its combat ranks and HHS about whether it's sometimes okay to be violent toward women.)

According to a recent Department of Justice study, 27 percent of the victims of family violence between 1998 and 2002 were men. And the department's statistics reveal the welcome news that, along with the overall crime rate between 1993 and 2002, the rate of family violence "fell from about 5.4 victims per 1,000 to 2.1 victims per 1,000 people 12 and older."[40]

This good news is unwelcome to the women who need a "national epidemic" to keep all those feminists employed. NOW argues for increased funding for VAWA to address the "growing problem of gender-based violence" and dramatically increases the number of victims by heading to high school on a hunt for male abusers. They allege, "Nearly one in three high-school-age women experience some type of abuse—whether physical, sexual, or psychological—in their dating relationships."[41] "Psychological"? That ridiculously expansive definition of "abuse" could apply to all teenage dating relationships.

Over the past ten years, hundreds of millions of federal dollars have funded an ideological crusade against men and marriage in the name of helping victims of abuse. VAWA doesn't promote reconciliation, or provide help for abused men or services for abusive women. In design and operation it aims to batter men and proselytize women about the constant threat the men in their lives pose.

The University of Cincinnati female psychologists whose book declares that "all female-male relationships [are] more or less abusive" and "women's bonding to men, as well as women's femininity and heterosexuality, are paradoxical responses to men's violence against women" are grantees of the Justice Department and featured speakers at training conferences for police, prosecutors, and judges.[42]

The National Coalition Against Domestic Violence has affiliates in all fifty states and operates as the "official" voice on the issue of domestic violence. Its mission statement links "violence against women and children" to "sexism, racism, classism, anti-semitism, able-bodyism, ageism, and other oppressions."[43]

In 1980, feminist psychologist Lenore Walker wrote *The Battered Woman*, whom she defined as "a woman who is repeatedly subjected

to any forceful physical or psychological behavior by a man in order to coerce her to do something." The Battered Woman Syndrome, now an admissible defense in all fifty states, is her creation.
Walker once argued that the syndrome applied to a woman who
took out insurance on her husband, practiced target-shooting before shooting him while he slept, staged a burglary, and then
headed out to a disco.[44] Such is the influence of a committed radical feminist whose ideology is shared by an aggressive network of
publicly funded academics, therapists, counselors, and advocates.

When feminists carry on about the "home" being the most dangerous place in the world for women, they want to create the image
of a white picket fence on a suburban cul-de-sac with a violent husband pacing around the family room. In fact, "Divorced, separated
and never-married women are victims of violence four or more
times as often as married women."[45]

And children are safest when they live with their married biological parents. Maggie Gallagher explains, "[T]he most likely person to abuse a child physically is a single mother. The most likely
person to abuse a child sexually is the mother's boyfriend or second
husband . . . [One study] found that a preschooler not living with
both biological parents is forty times more likely to be sexually
abused."[46]

In her memoir, published in 2000, Betty Friedan charged that
her husband of over twenty years abused her. She talked about "allowing Carl to smack me around," and stated, "It seemed as though
I never went on a television show in those days without a black eye
I had to cover with makeup." Her eighty-year-old former husband
was outraged over the charge and set up a Web site to defend himself. He wrote, "I have not lived 80 years of an honorable life to
have it trashed by a mad woman. . . . I've been divorced from her
for 30 years and still she haunts me and disrupts my life. I must have
committed some heinous crimes in a previous life to be cursed so."

Betty Friedan backed away from her charges. "My husband was no wife beater and I was no passive victim of a wife beater. We fought a lot, and he was bigger than me."

Carl Friedan still calls himself a feminist, but says, "I would just advise a person not to marry one."[47] No kidding.

2 | Day Care Good; Mother Bad

The feminist movement has long been on a collision course with what we know to be true about the natural bond between mother and child. The denial-of-differences version of women's equality demands that women want what men want and be every bit as committed to careers as men are, but biology won't let them have their win. Women fall madly in love with their babies in a way that devoted fathers don't. French feminist Simone de Beauvoir honestly confronted this obstacle to the feminist project when she argued that "women shouldn't have that choice [to stay home], precisely because if there is such a choice, too many women will make that one." How can mothers hope to achieve their 50 percent share of everything available in a man's world if once a baby arrives they fall prey to the dreaded Gender Stereotype and 100 percent of their devotion suddenly belongs to a child? Women would have to be snookered to leave their young children in the care of someone else. Proponents of the male model of career success for women and substitute care for young children—typically working mothers themselves—use subterfuge and censorship to thwart the free choice de Beauvoir feared.

Betty Friedan told American women there was only one way to avoid being a nonentity when she wrote, "But even if a woman does not have to work to eat, she can find identity only in work that is of real value to society—work for which, usually, our society pays."[1]

WHO REMEMBERS MAMA?

Cultural and economic forces have to be marshaled to convince mothers that they dare not rely on their husbands for support or sacrifice their careers in order to care for children at home. No less an authority that Supreme Court justice Ruth Bader Ginsburg thinks women ought to wise up to the patriarchal plot afoot. She has declared, "Motherly love ain't everything it has been cracked up to be. To some extent it's a myth that men have created to make women think that they do this job to perfection."[2]

Books are regularly produced by female authors, representing the Me-Gender of the Me-Generation, who insist that children's needs take a backseat to adults' desires. They follow a formula that rates rave reviews from the like-minded who apparently can't get enough of the familiar refrain. The authors counsel mothers to refuse to allow their children to interfere with their lives. Children, we are told, are endlessly resilient and will be happy as long as Mom is fulfilled. These proselytizing moms claim America is a rotten place that doesn't help parents "balance" work and family the way all decent countries do, chiefly Sweden. And fathers should get with the program and do more dishes and diapers.

These propagandists always talk in terms of "careers" for women, reflecting their own fancy degrees and cushy lifestyles and ignoring the reality that the great majority of women who work outside the home head every day to plain old "jobs." As ex–*New York Times* writer Ann Crittenden summed up the attitude in *The Price of Motherhood: Why the Most Important Job in the World Is Still the Least Valued,* "Raising children may be the most important job in the world, but you can't put it on a résumé."[3] But even those impressive careers aren't all they're cracked up to be when it comes to meeting women's different needs. *The New York Times* recently reported on female dissatisfaction with their equal access to the executive washroom. Experts were concluding that the relatively low number of women at the top of the corporate ladder wasn't due to sex discrimination or even to the pressures from home. According to one, "Men will grit their teeth and bear everything, while women will say: 'Is this all there is? I need more than this!'"[4]

George Gilder, the celebrated author of *Sexual Suicide* and *Men and Marriage,* reminds us of what mothers who work outside the home are sacrificing when they subcontract raising their children to someone else during their formative years. "Only a specific woman can bear a specific child, and her tie to it is personal and unbreakable. When she raises the child she imparts in privacy her own individual values. She can create children who transcend consensus and prefigure the future: children of private singularity rather than 'child-development policy.'"[5]

In *The New York Times,* Elizabeth Crow, the former editor of *Parents* magazine, gave a glowing review to Joan K. Peters's *When Mothers Work: Loving Our Children Without Sacrificing Our Selves.* It is a "passionate and convincing study of American parenting," and a "smart, clear look at contemporary mothers' lives." Crow approvingly notes the author's passionate point of view: "Mothers 'should work outside the home. If they do not, they cannot preserve their identities or raise children' who are both independent and family-oriented."[6] This woman author isn't validating the different choices women make that suit themselves and their families. The only responsible choice is to work outside the home and give your child the "benefit" of substitute care.

In her "ain't nobody happy if working mom's not happy" book, Peters's bias in favor of careerists is clear. She can't imagine why a woman might freely choose to put a career on hold to mother full-time, so she sees the choice as reflecting a fearful dread or damaged ego. In Peters's world, stay-at-home moms are timid and fearful.

Peters condescendingly claims that many mothers who choose to stay home with their young children retreat to the "kinder, gentler (and safer) world of motherhood," because they "are still deeply ambivalent about independence and success in the 'harsh' world of business." In fact, knowing that they would leave the workforce once they were mothers "made their independence more of a game than a real commitment and thus rendered it less frightening." Peters believes these women were playing "work" like they once played house.[7]

And according to Peters, women who prefer to be home full-time are hurting their children because "Children flourish with multiple attachments. Far from depriving them of full-time mothers, maternal employment creates an opportunity for children to form other close connections—not only with their fathers but with a network of caring adults who can both diffuse and reinforce maternal love, *relieving it of the isolation, self-abnegation, and involution that too frequently have given it unhappy and sometimes tragic dimensions* [italics mine, obviously]."[8] She has clearly spotted the hidden dark side of Donna Reed: the guilt of the stay-at-home mother!

Peters does allow that forming these enriching multiple attachments can be rocky. She recounts that when their babysitter, Rosa, who had cared for her daughter since she was three months old, took off for two months to visit her family in Puerto Rico, "our usually sunny, nonviolent three-year-old sobbed constantly, ran and hid under the bed if we tried to comfort her, and hit and rejected the replacement sitter and her beloved grandmother. In her sleep she cried out Rosa's name, repeating it like a Greek lament, in a widow's soul."[9] Peters cites a New York City psychologist who explained that parents should remain calm, allow the child to have her feelings, and then, "slowly, over a month or two, they will integrate the loss." The female shrink also helpfully reminds parents "that a child's life does not have to be perfect."

Peters notes that "mastering this loss can turn out to be a meaningful growth experience for children and parents." She wonders if her daughter's two-month "nervous breakdown" (as she and her husband called it) might have been less intense if they had "dispersed the mothering among two different caregivers. With a parenting network of several loving othermothers, no one loss, whether of a baby-sitter or a family care provider, would be devastating."[10]

Peters's book should bear a warning label to prevent any caring mother from taking her advice seriously, but at least helps to spare us her destructive advice by making ridiculous assertions that reflect a willful blindness to the most elementary characteristics of children. She ludicrously declares, "Children want mothers who take care of their own needs and who remain a part of the world." In fact, every mother in the audience ruefully recognized the truth expressed by the frustrated mother in Nora Ephron's film *This Is My Life*. The divorced mother's daughters object when she finally achieves her dream of becoming a stand-up comic. Her boyfriend advises that her children will learn to understand her needs: "You had to travel. It's part of your work. Look, kids are happy when their mother is happy." But Mom knows better: "No they're not. Everybody says that, but it's not true. Kids are happy if you're there. You give kids a choice, your mother in the next room on the verge of suicide versus your mother in Hawaii in ecstasy, and they choose suicide in the next room. . . ."

Peters's classic case for careerist mothers is made with silly assertions backed up by a collection of anecdotes. The problem is sexism—"both women and men have to overcome the limitations of gender training to modernize mothering"—and the answer is Sweden—"men have to do half the child care, and schools should be better, work more humane, and child care subsidized."[11]

New York Times editor Susan Chira's "splendid" book won a rave review from feminist Carol Tavris even though she allowed that she was weary of arguments making a case for working mothers that she sees as well-settled. "Do we really need to be shown again that time spent with children is not the ultimate measure of good motherhood?" But Tavris welcomes Chira's effort and agrees that "it's time to drop that tired, unanswerable question—'does working harm children?'—and move to the more important one: how can we make sure it doesn't?" Hint: Sweden.[12]

Chira, the *Times*'s deputy foreign editor, who as a reporter covered child care, claims there is a backlash against working mothers in *A Mother's Place: Taking the Debate About Working Mothers Beyond Guilt and Blame*. Pregnant with her first child, and planning to return to work after a six-month leave, Chira loaded up with the "baby care bibles" but "found little comfort in the pages of most of these books." She reviews the opinions of the big guns on child development, like Benjamin Spock and T. Berry Brazelton, who warn about the dangers of substitute care for very young children, before she dismisses such concerns as "typical of a dismissive and punitive attitude toward women that runs through psychology in general."[13] She allows that research does raise alarming questions about the effect of day care on young children, and notes that "most child care in the United States is poor to mediocre." She proposes a universal government program with mandatory national standards and regulations. Sweden![14]

For the record, tax rates in Sweden are 50 percent higher than in the U.S., no net jobs have been created in the private sector since 1950, and over half of Swedish children are born out of wedlock.

Of course, this tired recommendation is not what parents want, as Chira acknowledges when she writes, "Most polls show that many Americans continue to believe that mothers should not work if their children are younger than six; nearly half of those surveyed believe that to do so harms young children." And, she notes the class differences between those who rally mothers to put themselves first and less affluent mothers with small children. "[P]olls have also shown a divide between college-educated women, who usually prefer to work and raise children, and hourly employees, who would stay home if they were given a choice."[15]

So who exactly benefits from the expensive federal day care system she advocates? More affluent families, who can afford to pay for their child care, or those blue-collar mothers who have to work, but who don't want center-based care? Even when they pay lip service to allowing women choices, authors such as Chira never offer alternatives to help mothers who choose to stay home. Conservatives back tax credits for children that would ease the financial burden on all families with young children and that would be neutral about the choices families make.

Advocates of the male model of employment insist that public policy make it easier for women to head to work directly after school and react with horror at the notion of a female model that sequences raising families and being in the paid labor force, although that might be better suited to women's priorities and desires. Professor Neil Gilbert of the University of California, Berkeley, points out that baskets of benefits like parental leave, longer school days, and family allowances, sold as "family-friendly," typically reinforce female labor force participation and so should be more accurately labeled "market friendly."[16]

HILLARY'S VILLAGE

Chira's book was well timed. In 1998, President Bill Clinton proposed a $22 billion federal day care program to address what Hillary Clinton was reduced to calling a "silent crisis" because there was no evidence that working parents were clamoring for the plan. At the time, more than three quarters of pre–school-age children had mothers who didn't work outside the home, or only worked part-time. Relatives took care of roughly half the young children whose mothers did work. Controlling for inflation, the cost of day care hadn't increased over the past twenty years, and the majority of working parents reported they were satisfied with the child care their children received. With eight out of ten small children cared for by family members, it was unsurprising that only 13 percent of parents said finding child care was a "major problem."

Polls showed that what working parents wanted was to work fewer hours in order to be able to spend more time with their children. A 2005 survey of working mothers found that only 10 percent would choose to work full-time, while 30 percent would prefer to remain at home, and 59 percent would like part-time work.[17] But the Clintons' proposal had nothing to do with what's good for children or desired by parents. Hillary Clinton really does believe that "it takes a village to raise a child"—but her village is not populated with friends and relatives. "Experts" are the village elders. The most direct benefits in the Clinton proposal would go to the day care lobby, the National Education Association, big business, and affluent career women.

It included a $7.5 billion increase for the child-care block grant to the states, a $5.2 billion addition to the dependent care tax credit to subsidize largely center-based care, $500 million for tax credits for employers, $6.8 billion for new and old early childhood education programs, and $800 million to professionalize day care workers. Presumably, a noisy crisis would have demanded even more spending.

With no evidence that the public was demanding this spending on day care special interests, it became evident that the initiative reflected the personal-ordeal paradigm that frequently shapes Washington's public policy. Washington, D.C., has the country's highest percentage of families with both parents working.

And female members of Congress are naturally among the most single-minded, ambitious women in the country. During a radio debate in 1998, Congresswoman Ellen Tauscher (D–CA) told me that she enthusiastically supported the Clinton day care scheme because when she had a premature baby a few years before she had some trouble finding a babysitter. Mrs. Tauscher was elected to Congress in 1996, spending $1.7 million of her own money to defeat an incumbent Republican. With a small fraction of her personal wealth she could have hired a neonatal team from San Francisco General to care for her child, but she believed that her personal situation bolstered the case for expensive, federalized day care.

The majority of families with children wouldn't get a dime of the funds proposed, because, to the militant irritation of the day care industry, they don't use professional substitute care. The plan would have less affluent one-earner families, with median incomes of $39,000, subsidizing the day care costs for generally more affluent two-earner families, with median incomes of $58,000.

To lay the groundwork for the plan Hillary Clinton organized a White House Conference on Child Care in October 1997 with satellite links to one hundred sites around the country. A sense of panic about the plight of children pervaded the high-tech event. HHS secretary Donna Shalala declared that anxious parents wanted to know about day care, "Can I find it? Can I afford it? And can I trust it?" A NBC/*Wall Street Journal* poll earlier that year had asked Americans to name the two or three most important issues that they would like to see the federal government do something about. One percent said day care.

Within a month of the White House's big kickoff for the plan advocates like Joan Peters and Susan Chira called for, one of its interns became world famous, and Bill Clinton was too busy fighting for his own job to worry much about jobs for day care workers.

Hillary Clinton's day care scheme reflected the conviction of influential feminist academics, like Professor Gretchen Ritter, who think that stay-at-home moms are dangerous subversives. Professor Ritter has been a fellow at Princeton University and at Harvard Law School. She has been awarded a National Endowment for the Humanities fellowship and directs the Women's Studies Program at the University of Texas. Professor Ritter writes that women at home with children are shirking their responsibility "to contribute as professionals and community activists," which "is an important part of citizenship . . . something we should expect of everyone." She continues, "Full-time mothering is also bad for children. It teaches them that the world is divided by gender." And her radical egalitarian sensibilities are deeply offended by moms raising their own children at home, because this "privileges certain kinds of families. The more stay-at-home mothers there are, the more schools and libraries will neglect the needs of working parents, and the more professional mothers, single mothers, working-class mothers, and lesbian mothers will feel judged for their failure to be in a traditional family and stay home with their children." Apparently, only mothers at home can be harshly judged.[18]

In 1999, a day care study was released that purported to find no difference in the well-being of children based on whether their mothers were at home or worked full-time. As such "good news" studies typically do, this one received plenty of media attention. *The Boston Globe* reported: STUDY SAYS WORKING MOTHERS DON'T CAUSE CHILDREN HARM. The AP's headline tracked with this conclusion: WORKING MOM ABSENCES SAID UNHARMFUL. The media attention included a segment on CNN's *Crossfire* where I was substituting as the host on the right for a debate between Phyllis Schlafly and Eleanor Smeal. Unlike *The Boston Globe* and AP reporters who had told Eleanor what she wanted to hear, I had carefully read the study and found that you could make no such general conclusion.

The study didn't distinguish between mothers who worked only a few hours a week and those who worked full-time. The population studied had a median income of only $20,000 and was disproportionately minority and unmarried. The emotional state of children in the study was based largely on what mothers told interviewers. The latest study contradicted six previous studies that relied on the same database.

I tried to get Smeal to recognize that polls show mothers with young children would prefer to stay home with them, but she was having none of it. She ridiculously claimed that 70 percent of women work because if they didn't "they would sink into poverty." (Remember: The median yearly income for one-earner families is $39,000.) When I asked her if she agreed that care by parents is better than care by a stranger, she answered, "I think it is a combination of caring parents and good early childhood education."[19]

And what did she think was so crucial for very young children to learn that a parent couldn't teach them? "How to play with other children," she lamely replied. Schlafly made the point that babies want a secure attachment to a single person, and Smeal retorted that "We also know that one- and two-year-olds love and get along very well in groups." I pointed out that "Two-year-olds don't get along in groups at all," adding, "Two-year-olds get along like we do."

Smeal stubbornly refused to recognize that some mothers freely choose to stay at home, that many others would like to, and that parents don't want the government-run programs for toddlers she advocates. Her performance reflects the feminists' conviction that unless small children are weaned from their mothers' care, there will never be a gender-blind nirvana of equality in the workplace. They are waging an ideological campaign that assaults the primacy of parents in raising their children and that refuses to acknowledge any conflict between motherhood and career.

The late cultural historian Christopher Lasch wrote, "A feminist movement that respected the achievements of women in the past would not disparage housework, motherhood or unpaid civic and neighborly services. It would not make a paycheck the only symbol of accomplishment. . . . It would insist that people need self-respecting honourable callings, not glamorous careers that carry high salaries but take them away from their families."[20]

From its earliest days, the women's movement wanted to collectivize the nurturing of children and quite openly admitted the transformative possibilities of such a regime.

The 1970 White House Conference on Children became a vehicle for this brave new world. The delegates concluded, "we do not favor any particular family form," because "children can and do flourish under many other family forms than the traditional nuclear structure." Parents were clearly seen as dispensable. "The place where care is given is not the most significant dimension for the child. . . . The issue is the kind of care given, how this is handled, what abilities are nurtured, what values are learned, and what attitudes toward people are acquired."

Congresswoman Bella Abzug (D–NY), a delegate to the Conference, saw the possibilities if only America could be persuaded to embrace this radical social engineering. She envisioned "a child care system that would accommodate rich and poor alike, that would let our kids grow up with a chance to know each other and to learn to bridge the racial and economic gap that divides their parents." The final report declared, "Day care is a powerful institution. A day care program that ministers to a child from six months to six years of age has over 8,000 hours to teach him values, fears, beliefs, and behaviors."[21]

Sylvia Ann Hewlett and Cornel West, two liberal academics, recognized this antipathy in the book they co-authored, *The War Against Parents*. They explained, "Important strands of liberal thinking are antagonistic to the parenting enterprise. Scratch the surface and you will find that many folks on the left don't particularly like marriage or children. In their view, the enormous quantity of other-directed energy absorbed by families gets in the way of freedom of choice, and ultimately of self-realization. This is particularly true for women, which is why some radical feminists tend to see motherhood as a plot to derail equal rights and lure women back to subservient, submissive roles within the family."[22]

Hewlett and West forthrightly state, "As recent beneficiaries of liberation movements (feminist and black), we find it particularly hard to face the bare truth: children deserve primary time and attention and need to sit in the center of life. This is bound to curtail some of our hard-won freedoms. So be it. At least for the sweet, short years of childhood, everything else in a parent's life should be negotiable."[23]

Debates over day care—usually dubbed "the Mommy Wars"—are among the most treacherous fought out in the public square. In addition to being loaded with judgments about what mothers should and shouldn't be doing, the child-care establishment (an industry worth $36 billion a year) has engaged in deceit and censorship to prevent an honest assessment of what decades of research can now tell us about the effects of substitute care on children. Former CBS reporter Bernard Goldberg explains why female reporters, editors, and producers champion any apparent evidence that day care poses no problems for children. He says, "America's news-rooms are filled with women who drop their kids off someplace be-fore they go to work or leave them at home with the nanny. These journalists are not just defending working mothers—they're de-fending themselves."[24]

Hypocrisy is clear when liberal proponents of center-based child care are found advocating the boosting of big business's prof-its, the expansion of tax cuts for the rich, and the sabotaging of women's choices.

DAY CARE DECEIT

A few years ago, the whole sorry story was convincingly told by Brian C. Robertson in *Day Care Deception: What the Child Care Establish-ment Isn't Telling Us*. Robertson details the consistent research findings showing that day care is physically and emotionally harmful and explains that only a few brave experts have been willing to risk the wrath of the day-care establishment and liberal elites by talking about this evidence. One of them is Dr. Burton White, the best-selling expert on the first three years of life, who continues to plead with mothers not to delegate the care of their young children to anyone else, because "babies form their first human attachment only once. Babies begin to learn language only once. . . . The outcomes of these processes play a major role in shaping the future of each child."[25]

More typical than Dr. White is Dr. Benjamin Spock, who, after frankly informing 1950s mothers that day nurseries are "no good for infants," deleted this advice from 1990s editions of his manual *Baby and Child Care*, which has sold millions. He explained that such advice would make working mothers feel guilty, and he recognized they were heading to work regardless. Spock admitted: "It's a cowardly thing that I did; I just tossed it in subsequent editions."[26]

Feminist intimidation has created plenty of cowards. One child psychiatrist writes, "Some of my colleagues have told me they are reluctant to publicly voice their concerns about child care because they fear they will be seen as advocating the return of mothers to full-time home duty."[27]

In 1977, researcher Selma Fraiberg argued that even high-quality day care is harmful because it prevents children from forming the healthy attachment to one caregiver that allows them, in turn, to form lasting commitments as adults. Her book *Every Child's Birthright* was attacked for promoting an agenda that was off-message for the feminist project. But the bad news kept coming. That same year, the unwelcome results were in on a pilot program at Yale University that had been designed to provide the optimal day-care setting. The researchers concluded: "Group care, even under the best circumstances, is stressful for very young children."[28]

According to a study by the American Academy of Family Physicians, children in day care are eighteen times more likely to get sick than other children, and infants in day care have more than twice the rate of inner-ear infections as babies who are raised at home. At any one time, 16 percent of children attending day care facilities are likely to be sick. They are three to four and a half times more likely to require hospital treatment than children raised at home.[29]

By 1991, Dr. Louise Silverstein, who teaches courses in family therapy and the social construction of gender at Yeshiva University, revealed a most unscientific frame of mind by angrily writing, "Psychologists must refuse to undertake any more research that looks for the negative consequences of other-than-mother care." In an article in the *American Psychologist* that reads as though it were written for *Ms.* magazine, she declared that motherhood is an "idealized myth" dreamed up by men in politics and the clergy to "glorify motherhood in an attempt to encourage white, middle class women to have more children."[30]

Feminists insist that mothers of young children who work outside the home are an immutable "fact of modern life," and so have had to be creative to counter both parental instincts and expert opinion. They have dreamed up theories about the permanent speed-bonding that can take place between mothers and babies in mere days, and have argued (with no supporting evidence) that children cared for by their mothers alone are disadvantaged.

But government data show that families struggle and sacrifice to care for their young children themselves. In 2000, only 39 percent of mothers with children younger than three worked full-time and only 43 percent of mothers with children under age six worked full-time. According to the Bureau of Labor Statistics, 72 percent of mothers with children under age eighteen work outside the home, but almost a third of them work less than forty hours a week. These families with mothers at home either full-time or only working outside the home part-time don't reflect the "luxury" of having such a choice because they are affluent.

It seems there has been a welcome cultural shift. Many female graduates of the modern academy have escaped feminist indoctrination with their common sense intact. The workplace participation of married mothers with children under a year old fell from 59 percent (full and part-time) in 1997 to 53 percent in 2000, reversing a thirty-year trend. The number remained stable in 2002, and a Bureau of Labor Statistics economist called the seemingly modest decline "huge." Well-educated white women account for much of the decline.

According to *Time* magazine, 22 percent of women with graduate or professional degrees are at home with their children. One in three women with M.B.A.s is not working full-time, in contrast with just one in twenty comparable men. A survey of 1,263 men and

Day Care Good; Mother Bad |39

women born between 1964 and 1975 "found that Gen Xers didn't want to have to make the kind of trade-offs the previous generation made." According to one analyst, "They're rejecting the stresses and sacrifices. Both women and men rated personal and family goals higher than career goals." The magazine notes the speculation about attitude differences. "While boomer women sought career opportunities that were unavailable to their mostly stay-at-home moms, Gen Xers were the latchkey kids and the children of divorce."[31]

Mimicking feminist talking points, media coverage generally ignores the weight of the evidence about substitute care and focuses instead on the happier study results found in advocacy articles. When a comprehensive government-funded study clearly showed that longer hours in nonmaternal care correlated with behavior problems, it was argued that this wasn't a problem at all. Veteran researchers found a strong correlation between longer hours in nonmaternal care and "aggressive" and "noncompliant" behavior that included "temper tantrums," "demands a lot of attention," "bullying," and "gets in lots of fights." The study found that children in day care for long periods (more than thirty hours a week) were almost three times as likely to exhibit these problems as children with minimal time in substitute care (fewer than ten hours a week).[32]

Nancy Gibbs, writing in *Time*, gamely pointed out that demanding attention is a "healthy skill to develop if you are in a room with 16 other kids." One editorial optimistically argued that an aggressive kindergartner might grow up to be an aggressive CEO rather than an obnoxious bully.[33]

Peggy Orenstein, the former managing editor of the lefty *Mother Jones*, who frequently contributes to *The New York Times Magazine*, responded to the conclusions about day care and aggression by announcing, "A 1950s-style attack demands a 1950s-style response, which is why a lot of working moms last week felt the need to duck and cover." This strident advocate for mothers in the workplace offers her own possible explanation for the study. "Here's a theory: In a society in which working mothers are still viewed with ambivalence, perhaps their guilt and anxiety—even their resentment—is absorbed by their children and manifested as aggression." Sexism causes bullies! Of course, Orenstein also declares, "It is pathetic that in the year 2001 we have to remind people that two incomes are necessary for basic survival in most families."[34] We have to remind Orenstein that the majority of families with young children get by on only one full-time salary.

Dr. Sandra Scarr, a child psychologist, is one of the most influential day-care researchers and has published four books and over two hundred articles that amount to a massive corpus of propaganda. Joan Peters and Susan Chira, along with virtually every other advocate for "othermother" care, cite her research about the alleged benefit of multiple caregivers for young children. She argues that children have no particular need for their biological mothers and that the feeling would be mutual but for the cultural conditioning responsible for the maternal instinct.

Scarr has been on the faculties of the University of Pennsylvania, Yale, and the University of Virginia. In a conflict of interest that wouldn't be tolerated in any other field, she has published her academic work while serving on the board of directors of the largest day-care chain in the country.

Scarr believes, "However desirable or undesirable the ideal of full-time maternal care may be it is completely unrealistic in the world of the late 20th century." She proposes her vision of the "new century's ideal children." These children "will need shared care to develop essential social and emotional skills to deal with frequent job changes and relocations. . . . Multiple attachments to others will become the ideal. Shyness and exclusive maternal attachment will be seen as dysfunctional. New treatments will be developed for children with exclusive maternal attachments (EMA Syndrome) and those with low sociability." These aren't fringe views by a professional outrider. Scarr is a past president of the American Psychological Society.

Scarr parts ways with other feminists by condemning the policies Sweden (!) has adopted, like paid, job-guaranteed maternity leave and child allowances, because they "support maternal absences from the labor force" that are detrimental to women's careers. "Unequal child-care responsibilities lead mothers to be less invested in career development and less motivated to maintain continuous, full-time employment." Unlike Joan Peters, Scarr understands that some women actually enjoy staying at home with their young children. She explains that she is "really amazed at the number of young women today who are graduating from a very good university and who feel very strongly that they want to stay home with their own children because they are irreplaceable. . . . You need to say, why, why would children be better off if you stayed home and were miserable."[35]

MOTHERHOOD DEFENDED—AND DENIED

Daphne de Marneffe, a Harvard- and Berkeley-educated clinical psychologist and mother of three, has devoted a book to debunking the conviction that Joan Peters, Susan Chira, Sandra Scarr, Eleanor Smeal, and other feminists share. She writes, "The popular renditions of history of mothers suggest that what mothers want and need, what constitutes true equality, is to be freed from making the care of children central to their lives. Within this framework, it is almost impossible to understand the desire to mother as something more positive than fuzzy thinking, lack of self-knowledge, or weak politics. In other words, the popularized feminist conception of what mothers *want* [italics in original] is incomplete, and its biggest flaw may be its misunderstanding of maternal desire."[36]

It's de Marneffe's hope that the feminists she admires will come to realize that a sexist culture hasn't guilt-tripped mothers into leading miserable lives at home with young children. "[F]eminists concerned with the rights and opportunities of women can fail to appreciate the positive motivation—the authentic expression of self—that many women bring to the task of caring for their children."[37] She notes the influences on the young women Sandra Scarr despairs over. "Most women today are not struggling to break out of the ideal that instructed them to sacrifice everything for their children. They are more likely beset with the quandary of how to break out of the 'do everything' model so that they will have more relaxed time for their relationships."[38] And the unmet demand for Swedish-style universal day care? In de Marneffe's opinion, "Given how enormously expensive a government-funded day care system of highly-trained, well-paid staff would be, many people would rather put their money toward funding their own 'high quality' care of their children than toward a publicly funded system." She sees this public resistance as an expression of "the value people place on caring for their own children, and their desire to do it themselves if they can."[39]

Suzanne Venker, a full-time thirty-seven-year-old mother with two young children in St. Louis, Missouri, grew up with a mother who graduated from Radcliffe in the early 1950s and continued to work as a stockbroker after Suzanne and her sister were born. Within a few years, her mother quit and stayed home with the conviction that it was impossible to do justice to both jobs. Suzanne explains that her mother's experience and counsel convinced her to "sequence" rather than attempt to balance work and motherhood. After graduating from Boston University, she taught English for nine years before her first child was born.

In her recent book 7 *Myths of Working Mothers: Why Children and (Most) Careers Don't Mix,* Venker asserts, "Because of the widely held belief that a mother in the home is a woman repressed, our society fails to use common sense when it comes to the working mother debate." Venker brings a disarming dose of common sense to the arguments she forthrightly makes. She writes, "The reason the work and family balance continues to be elusive is not the insensitivity of men and employers, but that raising children has always been, and will continue to be, a full-time job. And no one, male or female, can successfully perform two full-time jobs."[40]

The myths Venker convincingly shatters include "Men can have it all. Why shouldn't we?," "You're so lucky you can stay at home," and "My children just love daycare." In an example of the maxim that we believe what we need to believe, Venker cites the enthusiastic mother quoted in one of the working mother polemics who proclaims, "Day care turned out to be an enriching experience for me and my son. At ten weeks old, he was coming home with artwork."[41]

If Suzanne Venker enjoyed the media attention lavished on proponents of day care and working mothers, her heartfelt view of motherhood would have resonated with the large appreciative audience she deserves. She writes, "Recognizing [the intense emotions that accompany motherhood] would undo all the hard work of the women's movement, because putting oneself first is paramount to their platform. Putting children first is considered beneath us as women. But loving her child more than herself does not lower a woman's status, it raises it. Motherhood elevates women, which is one of the intrinsic rewards of sacrifice."[42] *Glamour* magazine didn't ignore her book. In its monthly advice column on buying books, it was listed as a "Don't."

Sylvia Ann Hewlett met with feminists' wrath when she advised career-oriented young women about their motherhood options based on the experience of their older, and in many cases sadder, high-achieving sisters. She provided the medical details about the dim prospects of having children for women in their forties and highlighted the personal stories of successful career women who regret their focus on their professional lives at the expense of marriage and children.[43]

Syndicated columnist Molly Ivins was furious that Hewlett's analysis got attention in the media. She quoted Peggy Orenstein, who demanded to know how the sisterhood's censors let Hewlett's book reach such a large audience. She angrily asked, "Where were the women at *Time*? Where were the women at *Good Morning America*? Where were the women at *60 Minutes*?" Ivins claimed that the warnings were old news, but Hewlett documents how the information she covered was news to the young women she surveyed.

According to a recent Gallup poll, only 4 percent of adults will be satisfied if they never have children. In 2003, among childless adults over age forty-one, 76 percent wish they had children. One study showed that 88 percent of American women are unaware of Molly Ivins's "old news." They overestimate by up to ten years the age when female infertility begins. The most current studies show that female fertility begins to drop at age twenty-seven, and by age thirty can decline by as much as 50 percent.[44]

Joan Peters's bum advice for women includes, "I also propose that they consider having fewer children, later in life" because "equality means that women can no longer use motherhood as an excuse to drop out of public life and men simply cannot have it all."[45] Author Jennifer Roback Morse represents women who have wised up after mistakenly heeding the call of feminist sirens. She writes, "It took me an embarrassingly long time to realize that my two children needed me at home more than they needed anything my income would buy for them. It took even longer for me to realize that placing my intellect at the service of my family was a greater challenge than my ordinary life as a university professor. I had accepted far more feminist premises than I had realized."[46]

A few years ago, Hewlett conducted a nationwide survey of highly educated, high-earning women in two age groups. The "break-through" generation was ages forty-one to fifty-five, and their younger peers were ages twenty-eight to forty. Thirty-three percent of the high-achieving women were childless at age forty. Among those making over $100,000 a year, the childlessness figure rose to 49 percent. Back when these women graduated from college, only 14 percent said they definitely had not wanted children. There is little discrepancy between the "dream" and "reality" for their male peers when it comes to becoming a parent. Among high-achieving men, 79 percent wanted children and 75 percent have children. Of course, men have time on their side.[47]

Claudia Goldin was born in 1946 and was the first woman to receive tenure in economics at Harvard. Unmarried and childless, she told Hewlett about the "brutal trade-offs" faced by her generation of pioneers. Hewlett writes, "Depending on which study you look at, somewhere between 34 percent and 61 percent of high-achieving women are childless at midlife."[48] The older, high-achieving women who married, got married young. Only 8 percent got married for the first time after age thirty and only 3 percent after age thirty-five.[49] Hewlett quotes another pioneering female academic who calls childlessness "a creeping nonchoice."[50]

Over a quarter of all these women between ages forty-one and fifty-five said they would still like to have children. Eighty-nine percent of the younger high-achieving women believe they will be able to get pregnant into their forties.[51] Hewlett cites detailed medical studies and concludes that a woman in her early forties has, on average, a 3 to 5 percent chance of achieving a live birth through standard (expensive) in vitro fertilization.[52]

Hewlett explains that medical fertility experts launched an advertising campaign in September 2001 headlined ADVANCING AGE DECREASES YOUR ABILITY TO HAVE CHILDREN, featuring an upside-down baby in an hourglass. She notes that Kim Gandy of the National Organization for Women objected to the campaign. "But what Gandy sees as unwelcome pressure, others see as essential knowledge that helps women get what they want in life."[53]

While Kim Gandy, Molly Ivins, and Peggy Orenstein prefer to patronize women and believe that all sacrifices, however unwitting, are justified for career success in a man's world, Hewlett insists on exposing what she calls "a painful, well-kept secret" about the tough trade-offs older successful women have made to achieve equality in the workplace. "My concern is that many of today's young women seem convinced that their circumstances—and choices—are vastly improved." She believes this easy confidence is unwarranted.[54]

Women like Joan Peters, Susan Chira, Peggy Orenstein, Louise Silverstein, and Sandra Scarr, who condemn the social pressures that once inhibited women's ambitions in favor of staying home, now engage in a relentless propaganda campaign that dismisses the needs of children and ignores the natural desires of mothers. Under the banner of "choices" for women, they censor uncomfortable facts that inform women and leave many of them deeply regretful about the uninformed choices they've made.

3 | Skirting the Truth— Lies About Wages, Discrimination, and Harassment

Feminists have made the workplace worse by waging an ideological campaign to portray working women as a victimized class, discriminated against in pay and persistently preyed on by male oppressors bent on enforcing the patriarchy. Not content with the equal opportunity women presently enjoy, these women demand a strict regime to dictate wages and regulate relations between the sexes at work. Armed with distorted data and radical feminist theories, they reject other women's free choices and see potential rapists lurking behind every water cooler.

The persistent fable that women are denied equal pay for equal work has been a never-empty tank of gas that fuels feminism. Since the 1960s, when feminists sported 59 CENTS buttons, they have loudly claimed that the disparity in average wages between men and women is the result of rampant sex discrimination. The demand that people be paid the same salary for doing the same job, regardless of their sex, naturally enjoys broad public support. A sympathetic public is largely unaware that the claim that woman face widespread wage discrimination is a myth aggressively advanced by feminists.

Disparities in wages largely exist between women with children, and men and single women. This is not sex discrimination, but rather the result of choices mothers freely make in their desire to balance work and family responsibilities.

WAGE PROPAGANDA

When Katie Couric checked in with Gloria Steinem in 2005 to take a very friendly look at how feminism was faring thirty years after Steinem led her sisters into the streets, she lamented that women still faced gross wage discrimination (Katie herself enjoys a $65 million five-year contract with NBC). According to Couric, "While nearly as many women are now in the workforce as men they are still paid less. About 76 cents for every dollar a man makes. Up from 59 cents in the seventies." Showing that women clearly can do math, Steinem pointed out, "It will take, I don't know, half a century at that rate to get even to equal pay."[1]

Couric didn't identify her source. Molly Ivins attributes her 74-cent figure to a feminist outfit devoted to "pay equity." Ivins notes, "Equal Pay for Equal Work is the oldest demand in the feminist repertoire, and everyone gives it lip service; even the anti-feminists assure us that they certainly believe in equal pay for equal work."[2]

The allegedly discriminatory wage gap between working men and women was a pet cause for Judy Mann, *The Washington Post's* resident women's columnist, who specialized in illuminating all the facets of the victimhood visited on American women. In a typical example, she cited an AFL-CIO survey finding that equal pay was "very important" to 94 percent of working women. She went on to note that two out of five women saw salary as the "biggest" problem women face at work. Less ideological eyes might have seen that women believe simple justice demands they be paid the same as men for the same job. But that's not the lesson Mann drew.

She wanted women to get the same pay for doing *different* jobs than men. A proponent of "comparable worth," Mann persistently argued for a regulatory scheme that would dictate wages so that pay in fields with predominantly female workers would be comparable to pay in typically male occupations. According to Mann, it was a major injustice that social workers in Los Angeles, mainly women, were paid $20,000 a year less than probation officers, mainly men.[3] Another feminist lament on behalf of social workers compares them to highway workers, who make $1,000 more a year.

When Susan Bianchi-Sand, the former head of the National Committee on Pay Equity, compares these jobs, she commits a feminist fallacy: She assumes that women in traditionally female fields are underpaid because their occupations are dominated by women, and that there is little choice in the matter.[4] Even when working women's choices are acknowledged, Bianchi-Sand doesn't think there should be any consequences for different priorities when it comes to wages. "Yes, women leave at 5:00 to go home and look after their children. But they're still working, just not for their employers. Why should they get paid less?" she asks.[5]

A very frustrated Mann lamented, "Valuing women's work for what it is truly worth, compared with men's work, has been the toughest nut to crack in the modern women's movement."[6] She explained that unequal pay would cost a twenty-five-year-old woman $523,000 over her working lifetime, and she was a big fan of the Paycheck Fairness Act, sponsored by Congresswoman Rosa De-Lauro (D–CT). The legislation would allow punitive damages for violations of the Equal Pay Act. DeLauro's scheme was another jobs program for yet another feminist specialty. It would have provided for "education and outreach to encourage employers to assess their payrolls to make sure they aren't violating the law."[7] Under Senator Patty Murray's (D–WA) Fair Pay Act, employers would have to report their method of establishing wage rates to the Equal Employment Opportunity Commission.

In 2000, President Bill Clinton proposed spending $27 million to narrow the wage gap and wanted stronger enforcement of anti-discrimination laws in order to boost women's salaries. Alexis Herman, Clinton's secretary of labor, explained, "I have yet to go to the grocery store to buy a $1 loaf of bread and have the cashier look up and say, 'Since you're a woman, it's 75 cents.' Working women pay the same and should be paid the same."[8] Over half the states have considered legislation to remedy the wage gap.

The AFL-CIO's Karen Nussbaum and Linda Chavez-Thompson have devoted themselves to agitating for regulations to dictate employees' wages in the name of "pay equity." Every year an unholy alliance of labor activists and feminists promote "Equal Pay Day," to mark the date when women allegedly finally catch up—four months late—with what men earned during the previous year. During the sisterhood's 2004 celebration, Senator Hillary Clinton was on the bandwagon. She said the April date was "a day we hope not to have to celebrate again." Well, there is good news for Senator Clinton and the other wage warriors. There is no discriminatory pay gap between working men and women.

Since the Equal Pay Act in 1963, sex discrimination in hiring, promotion, or pay has been illegal. While there might be isolated examples of sex discrimination in the workplace, our competitive economy demonstrably provides equal opportunity for women. Here again, the wage warriors peddle victimhood and demand equal outcomes, regardless of individual priorities and choices. To make the case that women remain victimized, feminists point to average overall male and female wage numbers, or rail against a "glass ceiling" that blocks women's ascent to the top ranks of American businesses, or decry "undervalued" women's work that condemns women in predominantly female fields to toiling in a "pink ghetto."

The discrepancies in wages and occupations also fuel the feminists' insistence on affirmative action for women. Like so many other female scribes, reporter Rachel Smolkin of the *Pittsburgh Post-Gazette* cited job segregation as strong evidence of sex discrimination in 2001, writing, "Women make up only 1.3 percent of plumbers, pipe fitters and steamfitters and only 1.2 percent of heating, air conditioning and refrigeration mechanics. . . . These occupations offer men with high school educations well-paying opportunities that remain largely closed to women."[9] Feminist dogma demands that all discrepancies be seen as evidence of sex discrimination that will be eliminated only when women have parity with men in all occupations. So American women, the most accomplished and liberated women in the history of the world, need gender preferences in the twenty-first century in order to compete with men. Only preferential treatment will achieve the longed-for goal of having women make up 50 percent of plumbers or pipe fitters.

In addition to government regulation and government-enforced preferences, litigation is used to enforce gender parity on a targeted workforce. Wal-Mart is among the biggest targets. In 2004, a class action suit was filed against the huge retailer on behalf of 1.6 million current and former female employees that claims an insidious plot to keep them in their inferior place. If the class-action status of the case is upheld on appeal, it will be the largest private employment discrimination case in history.

The individual female plaintiffs who launched this sex bias case provided little evidence of actual discrimination, but a numbers game is being played, and the bean counters claim the disparity in employment between men and women makes the case that discrimination must be at work. *The New York Times* sees something seriously amiss because "about 65 percent of the company's hourly paid workers are women, but only 33 percent of its managers are."[10]

The non-unionized Wal-Mart has been named a "National Merchant of Shame" by NOW, although 66 percent of its hourly workforce and 80 percent of its department managers are women. In one instance, when the company advertised a management training program, 43 percent of the applicants were women, and 43 percent of those promoted were women.[11] Wal-Mart explains that although fewer women apply for management positions, women are promoted to managerial jobs at a higher rate than men.[12]

One clever critic of the suit points out the law firms representing the plaintiffs against Wal-Mart's very deep pockets appear to have gender disparity problems of their own. One firm that specializes in large class-action suits and calls itself "a leader in protecting the interests of men and women" has thirty-two male partners and only ten female partners. Another law firm involved in the suit has twelve male partners and only four female partners. Male associates outnumber female associates fourteen to eight.[13]

If it is true that women with similar educations, skills, and job experience work at jobs for salaries that are 25 percent less than men would demand, American employers are guilty—of violating the law of supply and demand. With a cheap female-only workforce, an employer could bury his competition. (For a time: the resulting competition would bid up the price of female labor until we reached equal pay for equal work—which is what we have now.) Recent Census Bureau data reveal that in 2003, college-educated black women, on average, earned more than college-educated white women ($41,100 a year versus $37,800).[14] The report didn't raise outraged cries of discrimination in the workplace in favor of minorities at the expense of white women. The uncontroversial explanation speculated that minority women tended to work longer hours, hold more than one job, and take less time off after having a child. These reasonable differences are dismissed out of hand when they apply to the wage gap between men and women.

In a classic example of how feminists ignore evidence that argues against discrimination in order to make the case that women face bias in the boardroom, authors Suzanne Nossel and Elizabeth Westfall devoted a book to the desperate plight of female lawyers. *Presumed Equal: What America's Top Women Lawyers Really Think About Their Firms* concluded that "systemic forces hold back women's progress and will continue to do so until institutional and societal changes are made," despite women's parity in law schools and success in landing top legal jobs. Yet in their own survey, women associates said that their prospects for promotion were equal to their male colleagues' "provided they [were] willing and able to put in the long hours and enormous energy." The attrition rate for women lawyers was admittedly higher than for men largely due to "the difficulty of sustaining a law firm career once one has children." The women surveyed by the authors showed "a keen awareness that the women who had achieved the greatest success in their firms did so at considerable cost."[15]

WOMEN'S CAREER CHOICES

Many of the women lawyers whose frustrated career aspirations were chronicled by Nossel and Westfall had clearly made decisions in their personal lives that naturally affected their lives at the office. These trade-offs between work and family explain some of the gap between the average wages of men and women and are responsible for the figures that purport to show a glass ceiling blocking women's career ascent.

These differences reflect, in part, the different priority men and women place on the demands of their families. In 1991, women without children earned 95 percent of men's salaries when other factors like education levels and experience were taken into account, but mothers, on average, made 75 percent of men's wages. Numerous other studies also find that although marriage didn't lower earnings, having children did.[16] Being a woman is not in conflict with having a demanding career, but being the kind of devoted wife and mother many women choose to be is. As law professor and author Kingsley Browne notes, "Those individuals, whether male or female, who are inclined toward competition, risk taking, and status seeking are more likely to reach the pinnacle of organizational hierarchies than those who are not."[17]

This commonsense explanation for career success hasn't derailed the "equal pay" agenda owing to feminist intimidation of anyone who dares to point out what we should recognize as obviously true. John Kerry's claim that full-time male workers made a dollar for every 76 cents earned by women for the same work was ignored by George W. Bush during their third debate in 2004. At a minimum, Bush might have pointed out that sex discrimination in salaries has been against federal law for over forty years and could have added that average wages don't reflect the number of hours worked or relative experience or the laws of supply and demand. When Karen Nussbaum declares, "Child care workers earn less than gas station attendants. We still undervalue women's work," it should be pointed out that women who choose to do so are perfectly free to take a less desirable job, like gas station attendant, in order to boost their pay.[18] But feminists resent the choices that women are obviously making. It is so retro for women to prefer doing the traditional work of women by choosing to care for children rather than pumping gas.

BALANCING COSTS

In a monograph chock full of data dismantling Judy Mann's obsession, Diana Furchtgott-Roth and Christine Stolba explain, "One of the greatest harms that the feminist movement inflicted on American women was to send the message that women are *only* fulfilled if their salaries are equal to men's and that a preference for more time at home is somehow flawed. Neither men's nor women's education and job choices prove social inequality."[19]

A recent study reveals that women have been increasingly looking homeward for their happiness, just as feminists have been peddling the message that women should count on the workplace for fulfillment. Between 1973 and 1994, "women have shifted away from finding work more satisfying than home toward finding home a haven." Women accounted for almost the entire increase of 31.8 percent to 40.4 percent in the "home-as-haven" category over those ten years.[20]

Unlike Rosa DeLauro and Patty Murray, who hype the feminist fable about wage discrimination to promote regulation of salaries, in *Why Men Earn More,* Warren Farrell shatters the myth of sex discrimination in salary disparities. He pays women the enormous compliment of assuming them capable of understanding the choices that affect salary rates and of taking lessons from the comprehensive jobs data he presents. Farrell provides far more help for working women than the wage warriors' agenda does.

Warren Farrell explains that in the old days, when he served on the board of the National Organization for Women in New York City, he proudly wore a 59 CENTS button, not yet wondering why anyone ever hired a man given that women allegedly worked at the same job for far less. He argues that other pay disparities exist that can't be attributed to sex discrimination. Farrell points out that there is a much greater discrepancy in average wages between never-married men and married men (62 cents to the dollar) than there is between women and men (80 cents to the dollar).[21]

Farrell began studying government data that refuted the feminist line. He learned that as far back as the 1950s, there was less than a 2 percent gap between the average wages of never-married women and men. Never-married white women between the ages of 45 and 54 actually earned 106 percent of their never-married white male counterparts in Lucille Ball's day. And, well over twenty years ago, men and women were paid equally when they had the same title and the same responsibilities.[22]

One can imagine how lonely Warren Farrell must have been feeling when, like a good feminist, he was claiming discrimination against women professors while working on his doctorate at NYU and discovered that women professors nationwide who had never married and never published earned 145 percent of what their male counterparts earned.

He figured the data showing never-married, educated women earning 117 percent of never-married, educated men reflected the superior ambition and work ethic of these women. But it wasn't just these educated women who made more than similarly situated men. Census data also told him that women who work part-time make $1.10 for every dollar earned by male part-timers who work the same number of hours.

While Farrell cites the most current possible data, he notes that when it comes to examining gender discrimination in the workplace, the books are cooked. "At this moment in history, gender-specific research is funded with a consciousness toward making women in the workplace look equally engaged but unequally paid." He explains that if studies focused on employment choices many women make, such as choosing flexible, fulfilling jobs, or working fewer hours, or being unwilling to move to undesirable locations, or taking more family leave, it would be clear that these personal preferences explain disparities in average wages.[23]

When Farrell helpfully turns his attention to providing advice to women looking to boost their earnings, he examines about two dozen causes of the disparity between average wages of men and women and highlights all the fields where women earn significantly more than men. The thirty-nine occupations where women earn at least 5 percent more than men range from aerospace engineers (111 percent of male wages), to financial analysts (118 percent), to speech pathologists (129 percent) and auto mechanics (129 percent).[24] Over two dozen college majors, including computer engineering, civil engineering, and history, will lead to higher pay for women compared to their male colleagues.[25] He cites a United Kingdom study that found the choice of college major explained 80 percent of the discrepancy between men and women's average wages. Farrell notes, "[T]he subjects most popular with women, such as literature and art, are also more likely to leave women unemployed and overeducated."[26] Women are fifty-three times more likely than men to get master's degrees in education rather than the physical sciences, and this number has increased over the past ten years.[27]

While it is true that women generally haven't been entering the higher-paid high-tech field in higher numbers, it's difficult to blame this on sexism when young black women are increasing their share of high-tech jobs.[28]

MEN'S DANGEROUS WORK

The feminist claim that the patriarchy segregates women in a low-wage "pink ghetto" overlooks the fact that while men tend to hold the highest-status jobs, they also tend to hold the lowest-status ones. Jobs held by women are, on average, rated slightly higher than those held by men. The *Jobs Rated Almanac* reveals that twenty-three of the twenty-five jobs rated as the worst are over 90 percent male. Men make up 54 percent of the workforce, but account for 92 percent of all job-related deaths. The most dangerous occupations include fisherman, logger, coal miner, and structural metal worker. They are all less than 10 percent female, with most of them less than 5 percent.[29] Every day in the United States, three construction workers die.[30]

Many men choose to take these dangerous but well-paid jobs, and many women elect to hold safer, more pleasant, but lower-paid positions. It has been shown that occupations that are more than 90 percent female almost always have such characteristics as physical safety, desirable or flexible hours, no obligation to relocate, and contact with people.[31] Even within occupations, sex differences in work preferences are apparent. Over 95 percent of nurses are women, but 42 percent of higher paid, and higher stressed, nurse anesthetists are men. Male doctors are more likely to specialize and to be in private practice, while female doctors tend to favor jobs as salaried employees. The veterinary profession is becoming predominantly female. Female veterinarians work fewer hours and are less interested in owning a practice than men.[32] On average, working men work about forty-three hours a week, while women spend about thirty-seven hours a week on the job.[33]

Farrell also highlights the unpleasant, high-risk jobs dominated by men that pay more than traditionally female occupations. "[W]e ignore a working-class man's equivalent of education: a willingness to risk his life in the death and exposure professions." He points out that men are about seven times more likely to die of work-related skin cancer.[34] After noting that jobs that are flexible, fulfilling, and safe typically pay less, Farrell explains that people have to be paid more to take dangerous jobs, reflecting "the death professions bonus."[35]

Men are greater risk-takers than women and tend to be more competitive and more interested in status. In a sign that Farrell has truly broken with his feminist past, he concludes that many ways to higher pay "are ingrained in male socialization. But they are also ingrained in male genes."[36] He does recommend that, despite the genetic heritage, our daughters can and should be encouraged to take more risks in order to boost their future earnings.[37]

Women are less than half as likely as men to work for over fifty hours a week. Working women are eight times as likely as men to spend four or more years out of the labor force, and nearly nine times as likely to leave work for six months or longer for family reasons. "Women, it turns out, are far more 'European'—working to live rather than living to work. But the glass ceiling is rarely cracked by healthy, balanced people who work to live," according to Farrell.[38] Farrell points out an important difference between men and women when it comes to the division of labor and balancing work and family. "It is not that men's underlying values were so different—they, like women, valued their family, home, security, and community. But men's focus on work demonstrated their devotion to their family, whereas women's focus on the family demonstrated their devotion to the family."[39] Since his feminist days, Warren Farrell has come a long way, baby.

BRING YOUR LAWYER TO WORK EVERY DAY

When feminists aren't maintaining that there are no differences between the sexes when it comes to work preferences or career ambitions, they are insisting that women in the workplace must be treated differently to account for their frail natures and special vulnerabilities. As Bernice Sanders, then at the Center for Women Policy Studies, complained, men didn't take sexual harassment seriously because they saw it as "merely pleasantries and teasing, whereas women see it as more threatening because men are in power." Here the difference between the sexes, denied in other facets of a woman's

job, are stark. One survey about men's and women's reactions to being propositioned at work found that 67 percent of men and only 17
percent of women would be flattered.[40] These different sensibilities
are highlighted by feminists who argue that whether or not actionable sexual harassment has taken place must be judged by a subjective
standard based on what a particular woman might find offensive.

When feminists recognize that women are particularly offended
by coarse behavior, they are adopting what they would screech was
a paternalistic view of the more vulnerable sex in any other context.
But the effect of sexual behavior on women in the workplace becomes a matter of sex discrimination rather than an offense to good
taste or the reflection of a coarsened society that affects men and
women alike, specifically owing to women's more delicate natures.

The sirens of sexual harassment hold that women heading to
work ought to pack a lawyer along with their lunch in order to be
ready to respond to any slight or slur. They sell women short. They
hold that women aren't smart and tough enough to flourish when
given an equal chance to compete with men.

The siren-in-chief on sexual harassment is Catharine MacKinnon, whose 1979 book *Sexual Harassment of Working Women* "approaches the status of scripture among feminists."[41] She was
co-counsel on the 1986 Supreme Court case that found it was sexual discrimination, and a violation of Title VII of the Civil Rights
Act of 1964, when a supervisor sexually harassed a subordinate
owing to the subordinate's sex. In that case the plaintiff's boss had
demanded sex from her, thus creating a "hostile working environment." Seven years later, the Supreme Court held that there could
be sex discrimination under Title VII even when the plaintiff hadn't
suffered economic harm.[42]

The prohibition on "hostile environments," enforced by the
federal government, has led to ridiculous censorship. The Kentucky

Commission on Women demanded that an employer change all of its MEN WORKING signs to gender-neutral warnings to avoid running a discriminatory workplace. Other agencies and courts have seen co-workers' use of "draftsman" and "foreman" (instead of "drafts-person" and "foreperson" if you haven't gotten the hang of this regime) as harassment.[43] UCLA law professor Eugene Volokh explains, "Without much fanfare, the law of 'workplace harassment' has turned into a nationwide speech code."[44]

Catharine MacKinnon's theory rests on what this famous theorist sees as women's essential powerlessness. According to her, "If sexual harassment expresses the pervasive reality of normal relations between the sexes, and if these relations express unequal social power, then the feelings and practices that emerge are not reasons that the practices should be allowed. They support and evidence the discrimination. Violations that would not be seen as criminal because they are anything but unusual may, in this context, be seen as discriminatory for precisely the same reason." There we have it. Normal relations between the sexes are discriminatory and should be prohibited.

MacKinnon explains, "In a patriarchal society all heterosexual intercourse is rape because women, as a group, are not strong enough to give consent."[45] Feminist poet Adrienne Rich also talks about "compulsory heterosexuality." Rich has been rewarded with every major literary award and was nominated for the National Medal for the Arts by President Bill Clinton in 1997.[46] Susan Brownmiller's 1975 book *Against Our Will: Men, Women, and Rape* notoriously declared that all men were potential rapists. These radical feminist views haven't been marginalized. They have been incorporated into sexual harassment law. When these women see an inevitable continuum from flirting to rape, any sexual overture from a man to a woman is cause for alarm.

POISONING RELATIONS BETWEEN THE SEXES

Daphne Patai is a self-described feminist who spent ten years in the world of women's studies. Professor Patai is alarmed about the "sex regulators" whose views have shaped current sexual harassment laws and whose main objective "is the dismantling of heterosexuality altogether." In her book *Heterophobia,* Patai faults what she calls the "Sexual Harassment Industry" that promotes a sterile world "in which both sexuality itself and the very fact of sexual differences are suspect, [and that] represents nothing so much as the ultimate triumph of ideology over humanity."[47]

She explains that feminist theory on the subject of sexual harassment clearly reflects the influential hostility of Catharine MacKinnon. "The feminist literature on these matters assumes that sexual harassment can never be accidental or trivial. It is always seen as part of a concerted effort to keep women in their place as an inferior social group. It is, so many serious commentators on it insist, an essential part of patriarchy's ongoing plot against women." Patai cites a typical example of the sexual harassment industry's handiwork in a brochure distributed on a university campus that explains, "Sexual harassment can be as subtle as a look or as blatant as rape."[48]

Time magazine quoted the assistant dean of student life at Vassar defending the promiscuous use of the word "rape" by accusers regardless of whether a rape had taken place. "To use the word carefully would be to be careful for the sake of the violator, and the survivors don't care a hoot about him." The female dean thought that men can benefit from being falsely accused. "They have a lot of pain, but it is not a pain that I would necessarily have spared them. I think it ideally initiates a process of self-exploration. 'How do I see women?' 'If I didn't violate her, could I have?' 'Do I have the potential to do to her what they say I did?' Those are good questions."[49] I have a good question. How have we allowed women who think that falsely accusing our sons of rape is a helpful exercise in consciousness-raising to wield authority on our campuses?

These sexual harassment specialists have been working on two fronts. They have largely succeeded in rewriting the law and now they have as their aim "nothing less than a restructuring of patterns of behavior, customs, and traditions—specifically, the transformation of relations between men and women."[50] According to Patai, a guide on sexual harassment on campus designed for administrators, faculty and students, co-authored by Bernice R. Sandler, represents a "bizarre propensity for reconceptualizing personal relationships largely in terms of power."[51] In her experience from her former days in women's studies, this animosity toward the natural affection and attraction between the sexes has had its intended effect. She says, "[Y]ears of exposure to feminist-promoted scare statistics have succeeded in imbuing many young women with a foreboding sense of living under constant threat from predatory men."[52]

In this guide, Sandler elaborates on what she views as the alarming "second stage" of sexual harassment, including "peer to peer harassment," which doesn't involve a superior/subordinate relationship, but which does fit the mandatory male-as-perpetrator, woman-as-victim formula. Patai rightly objects to the casual bias and the dismissive attitude toward basic fairness once a complaint is made against a putative male harasser. "In its nineteen chapters, hardly a line is wasted on the rights of the accused. This is no exaggeration. The word 'innocent' never appears in relation to any 'alleged harasser,' and presumption of innocence is entirely absent."[53] While false charges are never mentioned, the guide repeatedly frets about "reluctant complainants."

Elsa Kircher Cole, the University of Michigan's general counsel, contributes a chapter to the guide in which she explains what can be done about "apparent inappropriate behavior" even if a complaint hasn't been fully investigated. "The alleged harasser can still be confronted with his or her [sic] actions and warned not to continue them, and the harasser's unit can receive educational training about the institution's policies against sexual harassment. A sealed envelope can also be placed in the alleged harasser's file in the complaint administrator's office, not to be opened unless there are new allegations of sexual harassment against him or her [sic]." So the "sealed envelope" treatment and the reeducation regime can kick in when there is an allegation alone.[54]

While Daphne Patai devotes her book to the sexual harassment regime that has poisoned relationships between the sexes and unfairly empowered disaffected women on college campuses, the founding theory of these actionable complaints is in operation both in the university and in the office. She offers a thought experiment that sums up what feminists like Catharine MacKinnon, Adrienne Rich, Bernice Sanders, and Elsa Kircher Cole have wrought: "If 'sexual harassment' were relabeled 'female privilege' or 'demolishing men,' it would not command much support. If it were merely seen as a temporary wrong to be righted, and not as a dire peril stalking the lives of perennially beleaguered women, our whole social landscape would look different, hostility between men and women might well abate, and the [sexual harassment industry], finding small demand for its services, would wither away."[55]

The sexual harassment industry is not going to wither away as long as it provides thousands of jobs for its practitioners, despite having harmed the interests of women who must live with the poisonous atmosphere of resentment and suspicion it creates in the name of protecting them from the patriarchy.

FEMINISTS LOWER WOMEN'S WAGES

When the feminist lobby turns its attention to "balancing work and family" it also produces results of dubious benefit to women. Feminists who claim to be devoted to the needs of working women point to the passage of the Family and Medical Leave Act in 1993 as one of their most prized achievements. It was sold as a cost-free way to accommodate women faced with family responsibilities by mandating that workers in large firms be allowed to take time off, without pay, to deal with family emergencies. There are, of course, costs. Working women might be perfectly willing to make the trade-offs the mandate demands, but the trade-offs were ignored when feminists demanded the measure.

Under the law, workers in large firms trade higher wages or benefits for the mandated family leave benefit. If the benefit were free, employers wouldn't need a mandate to provide it. Any worker more interested in a longer vacation or better health benefits is disadvantaged when family leave is mandated, thereby reducing an employer's flexibility in accommodating all employees' requests.[56]

Mandated maternity benefits are not free. Women workers pay the cost of this mandated benefit. A study for the National Bureau of Economic Research found that the mandate lowered women's wages and increased the cost of insuring women of child-bearing age by as much as 5 percent. The MIT economist who conducted the study found that the wage rates of the targeted women fell by a dollar for every dollar of cost associated with the mandate.[57] A course in economics for feminists would be a cost-effective mandate that even this conservative could support.

One woman has done more to advance the financial independence of American women than all the theorists, academics, columnists, and counselors who claim the mantle of liberating women. When Mary Kay Ash died at age eighty-three in 2001, she left 850,000 sales consultants in thirty-seven countries with both the independence that comes from running their own small businesses and a philosophy of personal achievement that transforms lives. In 1963, after working for twenty-five years in the man's world of direct sales, one of the greatest successes in the annals of American business was born because Mary Kay, whose father was an invalid, didn't think that "God wanted a world in which a woman would have to work fourteen hours a day to support her family, as my mother had done." She didn't take to the streets, convene a seminar, lobby for legislation, or whine about the male patriarchy. With a $5,000 investment, Mary Kay Ash founded the cosmetics empire that now has over $2 billion in yearly sales. She launched her fleet of pink Cadillacs as the showy status symbols of her vision to provide women with an unlimited opportunity for personal and financial success.

Mary Kay Ash counseled that women could "have it all" if they prioritized their lives with God first, family second, and career third. I have witnessed her legacy firsthand. My sister Virginia Rowell is one of the company's most successful consultants. Hundreds of thousands of women have realized Mary Kay's dream for them. The charitable foundation she created raises money to combat cancers affecting women and domestic violence.

Forbes magazine named Mary Kay Cosmetics as one of the "100 Best Companies to Work For in America." She told an interviewer in 1994, "As far as I am concerned, our legacy will be that we have helped hundreds of thousands of women find out how great they really are. And that they can do anything in this world they want to do if they want to do it bad enough—and are willing to pay the price." She had a confidence in American women that their alleged feminist champions betray.

Unlike Rosa DeLauro, Patty Murray, Judy Mann, Molly Ivins, Karen Nussbaum, Linda Chavez-Thompson, or any of the other wage warriors who sell victimhood rather than empowerment, this entrepreneurial woman understood and respected the choices women make in balancing work and family. Unlike Catharine MacKinnon and Bernice Sanders, she recognized the sacrifices women willingly make on behalf of their children and the men they love.

4 | In the Classroom . . . Boys Will Be Girls

We parents of boys have meekly allowed gender warriors to treat our sons like unindicted coconspirators in history's gender crimes, while parents of girls permit their daughters to be patronized as helpless victims of a phantom, crippling sex bias in America's schools. Classrooms have been turned into feminist reeducation camps to stamp out all sex differences and smother the natural attributes and aspirations of girls and boys. When Gloria Steinem, who has raised neither, declared, "We badly need to raise boys more like we raise girls," she summed up the feminist conviction that boys' gender identity had to be radically re-formed. And the feminist reeducation project in our schools is determined to "free" young girls from their natural feminine traits. Our schools and universities are battlefields in a determined feminist campaign of indoctrination and intimidation, and students and scholarship have been the casualties.

Carol Gilligan is the most famous feminist theorist on the need to change the way our "damaged" sons and daughters are taught. Over the past twenty-five years, Gilligan, the first professor of gender studies at Harvard University, has inspired dozens of books and hundreds of feminist tracts building on her theories about sex stereotyping. Her writings are credited with making the case for the 1994 Gender Equity in Education Act, which banned sex-role stereotyping and gender discrimination in the classroom. The law has provided tens of millions in federal funds for the politicized research and strident advocacy of the feminist "experts" who define what the law means.

In 1996 *Time* magazine put Gilligan in the company of Oprah Winfrey and Vice President Al Gore as one of "America's 25 most influential people." The magazine asked, "How likely is it that a single book could change the rules of psychology, change the assumptions of medical research, change the conversation among parents and teachers and developmental professionals about the distinctions between men and women, boys and girls?"[1] In 1997, Gilligan won a Heinz award (yes, from John Kerry's wife, Teresa) for doing nothing less than changing "the paradigm for what it means to be human."

The book that made her a sisterhood star, *In a Different Voice: Psychological Theory and Women's Development,* was published in 1982, sold six hundred thousand copies, and was translated into nine languages. In the bestseller, Gilligan argued that there are distinctive masculine and feminine approaches to moral reasoning. Identifying a distinctly feminine moral sense with an emphasis on caring and intimacy in contrast to a male emphasis on abstractions and rules can be seen as an unremarkable reflection of the immutable differences between the sexes. But her feminist sisters adopted her argument about the sex bias in social science research, saw the prevalence of masculine forms of knowledge as oppressive to women, and resolved to transform education to eliminate "male-identified attributes" like "reason and logic" in favor of "feminine ways of knowing."[2]

Within a few years, Gilligan had decided our patriarchal culture silenced adolescent girls. Feminists swooned at the notion that as they entered adolescence, girls became aware that they threatened "male-voiced" society and so, as a matter of self-preservation, lost their own voices.

"I know what Professor Gilligan writes about," declared Jane Fonda in a speech at Harvard in 2000. "I know it in my skin, in my gut, as well as in my voice."[3] It might not be obvious that this infamous antiwar activist was too meek or intimidated to challenge the patriarchy, but Fonda explained that Gilligan's theories about speaking in "false feminine voices" "took my breath away."[4] In 2001, Fonda pledged $12.5 million to Harvard in Gilligan's honor to fund research on cultural assumptions about gender. Gilligan had already announced that she was moving to NYU, where she is now a professor dividing her time between the School of Education and the School of Law. Two years later, Jane Fonda exercised a woman's prerogative and withdrew her pledge. Fonda objected to Harvard's delay in setting up a new gender studies center, was frustrated at the inability to find a worthy successor for Professor Gilligan, and had seen the value of her AOL Time Warner stock head south after the announcement of her Gilligan gift.

But Fonda's largesse is hardly necessary to advance Gilligan's theories. The value of her withdrawn gift is dwarfed by the uncritical media attention feminists' politicized research enjoys and the wholesale adoption of their claims by the education establishment.

BATTLE OF THE SEXES IN SCHOOLS

In 1992, the American Association of University Women (AAUW) released a study conducted by the Wellesley College Center for Research on Women. *How Schools Shortchange Girls* was a media

megahit. It claimed that the widespread sex bias in schools damaged girls' self-esteem.

Peggy Orenstein, the former managing editor of *Mother Jones*
magazine, was galvanized by an AAUW survey that found an alarming crisis in girls' self-confidence. In collaboration with AAUW,
she haunted schools observing student behavior and in 1994 published *SchoolGirls*, which argued that girls suffer in classrooms at
the hands of both teachers and their male classmates. The male-
bashing, "gender-fair" regimes she promotes to remedy the allegedly
devastating damage done to girls' self-esteem are reeducation classroom camps for boys. She raves about a public middle school classroom in San Francisco presided over by an award-winning teacher
where women's pictures adorn all the walls and bookcases are crammed
with women's biographies. Orenstein figures that girls in the class
must be "dazzled" by all the female images and notes approvingly,
"Perhaps for the first time, the boys are the ones looking through
the window."[5]

By 1996, Mary Pipher's *Reviving Ophelia: Saving the Selves of Adolescent Girls* was number one on the *New York Times* paperback bestseller
list. A clinical psychologist from Lincoln, Nebraska, Pipher vividly
wrote, "Something dramatic happens to girls in early adolescence.
Just as planes and ships disappear mysteriously into the Bermuda
Triangle, so do the selves of girls go down in droves. They crash
and burn." Pipher calls American society a "girl-destroying culture."

Congress wasn't about to ignore the alarming press accounts
of schools shortchanging girls and the intense feminist lobbying
for a government response to the rampant sex bias that victimized
them. The special interest groups' studies were gullibly accepted, as
one AAUW advocate explained, because "They would not want to
vote against equity."[6] So in 1994 a law was passed.

Congress's resident feminists had predictably hyped their allies'
phony crisis. Congresswoman Pat Schroeder (D–CO) praised gen-

der equity in education legislation as a remedy for the Navy's Tail-hook scandal and claimed "we have studies that would fill this room showing that the young women do not receive the same kind of education or the same kind of treatment."[7] Olympia Snowe (R–ME), then co-chair of the Congressional Caucus for Women's Issues, explained that the caucus's efforts "were given new impetus after the release of a report commissioned by the American Association of University Women entitled, 'How Schools Shortchange Girls.'"[8] Senator Barbara Mikulski (D–MD) declared, "All of us are familiar with Dr. Carol Gilligan and her pioneering work. . . . Dr. Gilligan's research indicated that women speak in a different voice, but those voices are often made silent by the stereotypes in the dominant culture."[9] Congresswoman Patsy Mink (D–HI) wanted to make sure girls learned all the important basics, explaining, "Textbooks still ignore or stereotype women; girls learn almost nothing in school about many of their most pressing problems like sexual abuse, discrimination and depression."[10]

The 1994 Gender Equity Education Act identified girls as an "under-served" population in need of examination of their plight and classroom activism on their behalf. The Department of Education would provide millions to feminists to both study and remedy the alarming situation that inspired the law. The stakes in keeping the myth of crippling gender bias in our schools alive are clear. All that money for feminist activists would be in jeopardy should policy makers see through the feminist agitprop campaign and realize that girls are doing just fine in our schools.

Katherine Hanson was the director of the Women's Educational Equity Act (WEEA) Publishing Center, which was tapped by the federal government to promote gender equity teaching materials. Hanson is no education expert. She "trained as a journalist" and has made headlines as an activist against male violence. She rails against a culture that socializes boys to be "aggressive, powerful, unemotional, and controlling." Hanson blames a specific aspect of schools for promoting the male behavior she wants to eliminate: "One of the most overlooked arenas of violence training within schools may be the environment that surrounds athletics and sports. Beginning with little league games where parents and friends sit on the sidelines and encourage aggressive violent behavior . . ."[11]

Hanson's alarm about Little League is presumably related to her claims that nearly four million American women are beaten to death every year and that violence is the leading cause of death among women in the U.S. Such is the level of scholarship that passes for feminist expertise. The *total* number of female deaths each year is about one million, and the leading cause of death among women is heart disease, according to government data.

In Hanson's view, toxic little boys are the problem, and they would be the target of a relentless ideological campaign. Because feminists like Katherine Hanson and Carol Gilligan stubbornly believe that typical boy behavior is learned, they would be forced to unlearn it. Millions of parents can see their handiwork in classrooms where boys are diminished in order to strangle the "patriarchy" and boost the self-esteem of girls.

In 2000, Donna Shalala's Department of Health and Human Services announced that its "Girl Power" education kits were available for communities to use in order to address a pressing problem. According to HHS, "Studies show that girls tend to lose self-confidence and self-worth during this pivotal age [nine to fourteen], become less physically active, perform less well in school, and neglect their own interests and aspirations." There apparently wasn't much coordination going on in the Clinton cabinet. The previous day the Education Department had released its own report, *Trends in Educational Equity for Girls and Women*, which found that girls bested boys on every measure of educational achievement.

When my younger son was a third-grader in our local Catholic school, a story his classmates acted out one day reflected the feminist agitprop so widespread in our schools. As he related it, in "The Princess and the Dragon," the king's daughter complained that it wasn't fair the kingdom's girls weren't taught to fight. Her father agreed, and when a dragon attacked the castle, it was defended by the newly empowered little girls. "And what did the boys in the class do as the story was being told?" I asked. "Nothing," he replied. I have a vivid memory of the episode because it was the day I resolved not to delay in our intent to move him to a friendlier kingdom.

I had come to realize that our elementary schools are largely organized by women for girls, and too often boys are merely tolerated. We transferred John to the all-boys school his older brother attended.

At our parish school John was experiencing a gender-normed genre of current children's literature. In their attack on sex stereotypes in textbooks and readers, feminists have successfully created what Paul Vitz calls "Wonder Woman and the Wimp" stories. When Vitz, a professor of psychology at New York University, examined elementary school readers, he could "unearth no positive portrayals of motherhood or marriage for women" and in romantic tales, women often save men, but no man even tries to save a woman.[12] In a misguided mission to boost the self-esteem of our beloved daughters, we shouldn't permit schools to denigrate the admirable masculine virtues of our wonderful sons.

With the federal government's clout and cash, feminists have dictated the rewriting of textbooks to conform to their notions of gender equality. At its 1973 convention, NOW voted to take "dramatic action" to see that dangerous sex-role stereotypes were erased from textbooks, and within a year they had the Women's Educational Equity Act to advance their campaign with funding for alternative curricula. Tens of millions of dollars were now available for teacher manuals and instructional materials that adopted NOW's androgyny agenda. California, with its enormous clout in the textbook market, adopted a requirement for sex-neutral language, and its guidelines for textbooks demand that the contributions of men and women in history, in the arts, and in the sciences have to appear in equal numbers.[13] History is rewritten to achieve the Ms.-education of our children.

The editors, publishers, administrators, bureaucrats, and teachers' unions that make up the feminized education establishment eagerly adopted the gender agenda. Even in the absence of this politicized project, elementary schools are generally organized by women for girls. The chronic condition of little boys—once fondly recognized as "ants in the pants"—is now diagnosed as a disorder and medicated. The widespread misuse of Ritalin, prescribed largely to boys to treat attention deficit disorder, permits feminized schools to accommodate perfectly normal unruly boys. In grammar schools, competition and academic awards are increasingly out, and cooperation and sharing are in. But boys typically want to win, not share. Frustrated feminist experts see this natural aggression and competitiveness as a pathology and vainly hope early intervention will eliminate boyhood.

BOYS ARE THE ENEMY

After decades of "gender studies" depicting the woeful condition of young girls, researchers have now stumbled upon an obvious truth: it's a tough time to be a boy. In her best-selling book published in 2000, *The War Against Boys*, Christina Hoff Sommers dismantled the feminist education theorists with, dare I say, cool masculine logic. She points out that she is up against a federally funded "cottage industry of gender-bias specialists."[14] Since 1980, Katherine Hanson's outfit has received about $75 million in federal funds.

Though far outnumbered, Sommers is never outclassed, and her intellectual firepower is more than a match for the gender feminists whose academic handiwork she skillfully debunks—again, and again, and again. A senior fellow at the American Enterprise Institute, this former professor of philosophy respects first-rate scholarship and saw firsthand the shoddy advocacy research that has become a specialty of academic feminists. Her methods are dangerously subversive. She challenges feminist advocates to back up their anecdotes with social science research. When she spots an implausible assertion attributed to some research finding, she searches out the original source, examines its data, contacts the statisticians responsible, and sets the record straight.

When HHS secretary Donna Shalala, in 1993, touted a finding that 40 percent of American women are "severely depressed," Sommers went to work. She learned that according to government data, the yearly prevalence of severe depression is 5 percent for women. When she tracked down the analyst responsible for the grossly inflated number being promoted by HHS, the analyst explained that she wanted to make sure that her work countered the "phallocentric bias" that she saw in "white male norms" of research. What about the Office of Women's Health's claim that "an estimated 30 percent of emergency-room visits by women each year are the result of injuries from domestic violence"? Thanks to Christina Hoff Sommers's tenacity, we know the nationwide figure is closer to 2 percent.[15]

Her three books overflow with examples of the pseudoscience behind leftist advocacy. Sommers graduated Phi Beta Kappa from New York University and earned her Ph.D. in philosophy from Brandeis University. Betty Friedan dismissed her as "a lightweight and a birdbrain."[16] The charming and refined Sommers dismisses the ugly criticisms she regularly receives with a bemused detachment. Maybe feminists are upset that Sommers is performing a stereotypical woman's role by cleaning up after them.

In contrast to the emotional, anecdotal advocacy she convincingly debunks, Sommers uses solid social science research in making her case that an educational establishment committed to feminists' notions about gender equity is harming boys.

She points out that while Gilligan, the AAUW, Orenstein, and Pipher were all the rage, with the media in the throes of the "girl crisis" they had supposedly documented, serious scholars were soundly refuting their theories. For example, one consensus of experts in adolescent psychology had concluded in 1993: "It is now known that a majority of adolescents of both genders successfully negotiate this developmental period without any major psychological or emotional disorder, develop a positive sense of personal identity, and manage to form adaptive peer relationships at the same time they maintain close relationships with their families."[17]

And where was the evidence that girls were either "silenced" or suffering in America's schools? As Sommers explains: "Data from the U.S. Department of Education and from several recent university studies show that far from being shy and demoralized, today's girls outshine boys. Girls get better grades. They have higher educational aspirations. They follow a more rigorous academic program and participate more in the prestigious Advanced Placement (AP) program."[18] More boys drop out of school and get left back, and they are three times as likely as girls to be in special education programs.

A 1997 MetLife survey of over two thousand students and teachers in grades seven through twelve found: "Contrary to the commonly held view that boys are at an advantage over girls in school, girls appear to have an advantage over boys in terms of their future plans, teachers' expectations, everyday experiences at school and interactions in the classroom." Sommers cites some of the survey's specific findings: Girls are more likely to see themselves as college bound, and more boys than girls feel teachers don't listen to them (31 percent versus 19 percent). She notes that the survey, conducted by Louis Harris and Associates, was largely ignored by the media because "where girls are concerned, good news is no news."[19]

Sommers comes to her task with her own bias. The difference is that hers doesn't distort her research and is shared with the great majority of parents whose children are being indoctrinated with feminist ideology. Sommers, a mother of boys, explains that her book is "a story of how we are turning against boys and forgetting a simple truth: that the energy, competitiveness, and corporal daring of normal, decent males are responsible for much of what is right in the world."

Christina Hoff Sommers provides commonsense advice rather than politicized pop psychology. She writes, "Children need to be moral more than they need to be in touch with their feelings. They need to be well-educated more than they need to have their self-esteem raised. Children do not need support groups or twelve-step programs. They don't need to have their femininity or masculinity 'reinvented.'"

First Lady Laura Bush has echoed the need to pay more attention to the well-being of boys. The mother of twin daughters said, "I think we've paid a lot of attention to girls for the last thirty years, and we have this idea in the United States that boys can take care of themselves." If Mrs. Bush can persuade her husband's appointees to turn off the feminist funding spigot at the Department of Education, thousands of feminist education experts could get real jobs while the rest of us get to work kicking gender politics out of the classroom.

A comprehensive study of how boys and girls are faring, released in 2005, tracked both from childhood through their early twenties between 1985 and 2001. The twenty-eight variables on the "Index of Child Well-Being" covered seven broad areas. It concluded that the well-being of girls and boys has improved at about the same rate. Boys are more likely to commit crimes and be the victim of crimes, while girls are more likely to attempt suicide, but less likely to use alcohol or drugs. Girls are more likely to graduate from high school and college. NOW president Kim Gandy was despondent. "This reminds me of that saying 'lies, damn lies and statistics,'" she fumed. "There's no question that boys and girls have disadvantages in different ways, but the variables they have chosen seem designed to show girls are doing better."[20]

The mission of the Catholic all-boys school both my sons attended is to produce the kind of strong, virtuous men parents want their daughters to marry. The boys diagram sentences, memorize poetry (with competitive poetry drills), and study Latin. They read about soldiers, explorers, and Greek heroes. They pray together, have recess twice a day, play in the rain, wreck their good shoes, and regularly lose their jackets and ties. And they like school.

Sandra Stotsky, a research scholar at Northeastern University, was on the steering committee for reading assessment at the National Assessment of Educational Progress (NAEP), the comprehensive yearly analysis of student achievement. She cites an Education Department study of high school seniors that found girls lost two points in reading scores and boys lost six points between 1992 and 2002, leaving a sixteen-point gender gap.[21] Overall, boys' reading performance lags behind girls' by approximately 1.5 years.

A test of kindergartners in 1998 revealed that girls' reading proficiency over boys doubled between the fall and spring semesters. Stotsky believes that the feminized curriculum contributes to boys' relatively poor reading scores. "Publishers seem to be more interested in avoiding 'masculine' perspectives or 'stereotypes' than in getting boys to like what they are assigned to read." So, "Gone are the inspiring biographies of the most important American presidents, inventors, scientists, and entrepreneurs. No military valor, no high adventure. On the other hand, stories about adventurous and brave women abound." Although Peggy Orenstein would be delighted that girls rule on schools' reading lists, the result of all this "gender fairness" is clear. Stotsky says, "What was formerly a moderate difference is fast becoming a decided marker of gender identity: Girls read; boys don't."

For non-ideologues, there is no doubt that boys and girls are hard-wired to be different. Parents determined to provide their children with gender-neutral toys will despondently report that their two-year-old son makes gun noises while brandishing a crayon, or their toddler daughter lovingly makes a bed for her doll in the back of a Tonka truck. They learn firsthand what stacks of research on the brain reveal about sex differences.

Michael Gurian, in his book *The Wonder of Boys*, recounts that researchers at Johns Hopkins in the late eighties were treated with suspicion when their study of one hundred thousand boys and girls revealed that biologically inherited brain and hormonal differences basically control the way males and females operate. It is now clear, according to Gurian, that these researchers "have been more than vindicated."

Girls' brains are stronger in the left hemisphere, where language is processed, while boys' brains are more oriented toward the right hemisphere, the spatial center. There will be more female French-literature majors, and men will dominate engineering departments, despite the efforts of the gender police.

Ignoring the scientific conclusions, gender-blind zealots persist in their ideological conviction that sexual identity represents learned behavior. Feminists use the language of the civil rights movement, and male characteristics are likened to racist attitudes that must be stamped out. It is therefore as wrong to segregate by sex as it once was to segregate by race. So, although both boys and girls can benefit from single-sex education, it must be prohibited as discriminatory—a view adopted by Justice Ruth Bader Ginsburg writing for the Supreme Court in the Virginia Military Institute case. Discriminatory for some, that is. Ginsburg claims that women's colleges, unlike those nasty all-male schools like VMI, serve a vital function because they "dissipate, rather than perpetuate, traditional gender classifications." So, when it comes to single-sex education, according to Justice Ginsburg, what's good for the goose isn't good for the gander.

GIRLS WON'T BE GIRLS

What Christina Hoff Sommers did in sounding the alarm about the harm hostile feminists are doing to American boys, James Tooley did on behalf of British girls, who are being hurt by the same misguided campaign of sexual sameness. In *The Miseducation of Women*, Tooley notes that he is tackling the effects of a most unwelcome American export: "It's clear that where American feminism has led, the rest of the world has followed." Owing to the legal regime in both the U.S. and Britain, he explains, "A girl must be informed through all channels that her wishes and desires for her future life must be the same as a boy's."[22]

Tooley, a professor of education policy, explains why he is determined to see that young women be spared feminists' monolithic view of what is appropriate and be allowed to freely choose the education, marriage, or career path they wish for themselves. He cites Bridget Jones as the confused, unhappy offspring of feminists like Betty Friedan. In her 1963 landmark book *The Feminine Mystique*, Friedan recognized, "The key to the trap is, of course, education."[23]

Tooley believes that a representative product of the feminists' education project is the thirty-something heroine of Helen Fielding's novel *Bridget Jones' Diary*, who, like all her single friends, is desperate to find a man to settle down with. The book sold 4 million copies in thirty countries, and as further evidence that plenty of women identify with the desperate, disappointed Bridget, Tooley cites studies about the declining happiness of American and British women. One large study of well-being data on one hundred thousand Americans and Britons from the early 1970s to the late 1990s found that while American men had grown happier, women's well-being had dramatically fallen during the period. In the late nineties, women were almost 20 percent less happy than they had been over twenty years before. He notes that Betty Friedan and Germaine Greer have both been grappling with their own recognition that their early feminist theories have not improved women's well-being.

"We've swapped a society where women could be full-time mothers—a role many found fulfilling and satisfying—for one that fuels consumerism and clogs our roads with second cars on the drive to school, where spoiled children, buried under mountains of toys they can't be bothered to play with, watch suggestive TV shows in their lonely bedrooms. And we have this partly because the equality feminists forced us to believe that motherhood was parasitic, the housewife a leech."[24]

As a young academic, Tooley was a self-described feminist and worked as a researcher at Britain's National Foundation for Educational Research (NFER), where he was warned against writing examination questions that favored boys. He recalls that he and his fellow researchers recognized that what they called "gender-neutral" questions actually penalized boys. He began to realize that the educational establishment was brimming with acolytes of feminists like Friedan, who famously announced that women could only "feel alive" through paid work. He saw that schools were teaching girls that their careers were of paramount importance in their teens and twenties because feminists overvalue what men do at the expense of the female, creating a "masculinist mystique" that destructively devalues the home and family.[25]

Tooley recognizes that all women certainly don't want the same things, but points out that the happy home so many women actually do want, despite feminists' admonitions that they shouldn't, has been made harder to achieve thanks to feminists. "Perhaps the underlying problem with the traditional arrangements is caused by the feminist revolution that has liberated men to commitment-free sex and serial monogamy, and brought in no-fault divorce to complete their liberation from interdependency. If all this is so, you cannot make women more secure by further promoting their independence through schooling."[26]

"Girl-friendly" reforms in Britain attempted to eliminate the problem of gender stereotyping in the late 1980s by imposing a compulsory curriculum that permitted no choices in subjects for either boys or girls up to the age of sixteen. Tooley cites the findings of a government commission on the success of efforts to eliminate sex differences: "At all qualification levels, gender stereotyping of subjects is prevalent *wherever choice is allowed.*"[27] He points out that "30 years of gender reform may not be long enough to change human predilections," and figures it's time to test the feminists' assumption that men and women make different choices owing to socialization.

Tooley marshals persuasive evidence on the biological roots of sex differences in psychology, cognitive abilities, and emotions. His engaging review of the literature on evolutionary psychology includes fascinating examples of the differences between the sexes and explores the various theories that explain how the sexes evolved. He points out that much of what society values—art, language, and morality—appears to have arisen as the result of female regulation of male behavior.[28] Now, feminism encourages girls to behave as aggressively as boys. "Perhaps it is no wonder that we see a general decline in the manners and public behavior of boys and young men, who would be only too willing to be well behaved if this is what the girls were allowed to want from them."[29]

In a delightfully ironic point, Tooley cites evidence that the dreaded male patriarchy, which values status and achievement, might well have developed in response to what women wanted in their men. If women's preferences are responsible for the patriarchy, in what sense can they be said to be oppressed by it?[30]

Tooley concludes his appeal to allow women the free choices feminists claim to support by sounding call to listen to all women's voices. While feminists claim to be speaking for womankind, Tooley recognizes that he's not. He believes that women who want to should pursue nontraditional degrees and careers, but he wants the educational establishment to start hearing the voices of women who would benefit if schools recognized their desire for marriage and motherhood. He urges Congress and Parliament to knock it off with the gender fairness studies and stop worrying about too many girls studying hairdressing and too few majoring in math and the sciences.

"Above all, we should allow a thousand flowers to bloom here, to find what works best for girls and boys, and not assume that it will always be the same for each sex. Only that will enable boys and girls truly to flourish as individuals."[31]

PHANTOM PREJUDICE

Diana Furchtgott-Roth and Christine Stolba call women's remarkable educational success the "foremost example of the feminists' dilemma," because it forces them to flail around looking for gender bias where plainly none exists. On many campuses, women are the dominant sex. "Women are matching or surpassing their male peers in test scores and graduation rates, and no one limits women's choices of fields of study."[32] The AAUW has taken to talking about the "subtle gender bias" afflicting women. "Imaginary gender bias" is more like it.

Women have faced education discrimination in the past when they were prohibited from attending many schools and discouraged from pursuing many degrees. Still, since 1870, the first year for which data are available, women have made up more than half of all high school graduates. Women now receive 56 percent of all bachelor's and master's degrees, and their percentage of these degrees has exceeded men's share since the early 1980s. By 1998, women were receiving 42 percent of all doctorates.[33]

According to a report from Postsecondary Education Opportunity, a leading higher education research organization: "In the 30 (plus) years that we have studied education enrollments, we have marveled at the progress of females and become increasingly concerned about the lack of progress of males."[34] The report adds, "A tongue-in-cheek extrapolation of the long-term trend in the declining share of bachelor's degrees awarded to men indicates that the last male to earn a bachelor's degree will walk across the stage at final ceremonies in 2144."[35]

The authors of The Feminist Dilemma explain that feminists don't see their notion of equality in women's enormous educational success because they insist that discrimination exists if there are not equal percentages of men and women in all fields of study. They also point out the huge financial stake the feminist movement has in the publicly funded quest for "gender equity." Don't expect feminists to recognize the progress that would make their jobs obsolete.

Wisconsin's gender equity consultant explains that although women outnumber men in colleges, they are clustered in humanities, education, and nursing and so can expect lower-paying careers than the men who dominate computer science and engineering. Her reasoning ensures her job will exist in perpetuity.[36]

Feminists want engineering and math programs, for example, to be 50 percent female. They don't seem to care that men are underrepresented in nursing and dance programs. Girls are taking advanced math and science courses in large numbers. In 1985, girls represented 39 percent of students taking the advanced placement test in calculus. By 2000, girls represented 45 percent. In the same period the percentage of girls taking the advanced placement test in chemistry rose from 30 percent to 44 percent. On average, boys and girls perform equally well on such tests, but there are more boys in the small number at the very top, and more boys in the very bottom of test-takers. And more men major in engineering, mathematics, and physical sciences.[37]

Of course, sex discrimination is always in the eye of the feminist beholder. Equal opportunity, as the law and simple justice demands, is not enough. Only equal outcomes will satisfy the AAUW's vision of equality. When women choose to pursue an education in a traditionally female field, their choice is chalked up to a "false consciousness" that supposedly reflects society's debilitating messages. The authors of *The Feminist Dilemma* ask a good question: "If the social pressures feminists claim prevent women from entering math, physics, and engineering really exist, why do they not apply to law, biology, dentistry, and medicine?"[38]

Feminists persistently float schemes to address the rampant (though "subtle") sexism on American campuses. A few years ago, feminists at the University of Massachusetts at Amherst developed a program of mandatory gender studies they hoped to take nationwide. "Vision 2000" would include sensitivity training for all professors and students, and "women-friendly pedagogies" would be imposed in all classes. Penalties would be imposed on departments with high female dropout rates. Males could not be "overrepresented" in any curriculum. The sweeping plan represented the goal of realizing nothing less than a total feminist makeover of the academy. Its principles were approved for implementation by New England's six land-grant universities.

Ann Ferguson, director of women's studies at UMass, recognized that the proposal offended the principle of academic freedom, but explained, "We can't lose track of the wider goal in order to defend some narrow definition of academic freedom."[39]

There are about seven hundred women's studies departments and programs and thousands of individual courses devoted to the "women's perspective" in American universities. After reviewing these academic offerings, which began to be available in the 1970s, two disaffected feminist professors summed up their effect on women students: "Their sensitivities were being sharpened to such an edge that some were turned into relentless grievance collectors or rendered too suspicious to function in the workaday world outside of Women's Studies and were left with few possible roles in life beyond that of angry feminists."[40] There is, of course, a healthy job market for hostile feminists in women's studies programs.

Although feminist lore has it that the establishment of these faux academic courses represented a courageous feminist struggle to scale the walls of the patriarchal academy, 350 programs took root in the first decade of demand. The Alan Aldas of the American academy warmly welcomed their radical sisters to the struggle. The need for academic credentials was often brushed aside (so patriarchal!) in order to hire uncredentialed feminists who would enthusiastically realize the openly stated goal of creating the "academic arm of feminism."

CAMPUS INTIMIDATION CAMPAIGN

The familiar formula of grievance, therapy, radical politics, and disdain for conventional scholarship and academic freedom characteristic of the women's studies racket was on depressing display when Lawrence Summers, the president of Harvard University, was forced to make serial abject apologies and pay a tribute to his feminist tormentors. Summers had the temerity to venture the opinion that maybe, just maybe, sex differences in cognition explained the underrepresentation of women in science and math careers. At a small academic conference on January 14, 2005 (the date has become an inspirational battle cry for aggrieved academic feminists), devoted to examining how to diversify the workforce in hard sciences, Summers, an economist by training, offered three possible reasons for the sex imbalance in the sciences. He surmised that the demanding eighty-hour workweek in such fields might discourage women with children. Summers also made an economist's point: If women's underrepresentation was the result of discrimination, then a school that didn't discriminate would gain an advantage by hiring away top women who were discriminated against elsewhere.

Fatally, in a setting presumably conducive to academic debate, he also pointed out that more boys score at the very top on standardized math tests in high school and mentioned behavioral genetics research indicating this sex difference may not be the result of socialization. On average, there might be little difference between the sexes in intellectual abilities, but there are more males at the very top and at the very bottom, and Harvard and Massachusetts Institute of Technology professorships could be expected to demand evidence of performing at the optimum level.

Summers's suggestion that there might be some innate differences between men and women prompted a walkout by Nancy Hopkins, a biologist at MIT.

NOW promptly issued a press release calling for the resignation of Summers, "who has failed to lead the prominent (and previously all-male) university toward true inclusion of women." On behalf of the "women of Harvard," NOW president Kim Gandy asked, "How can they trust that Summers is committed to equality for women when he doesn't seem to believe that discrimination exists?"[41]

Of course, Summers wasn't saying anything about a particular woman or man's abilities, but feminists refuse to be deterred from pursuing their political agenda and so reject any evidence of individuals' different abilities and aspirations. Women's membership in an allegedly maligned group animates feminist politics. Within a few days, President Summers issued a "mea culpa" letter to "Members of the Harvard Community" stating, "I was wrong to have spoken in a way that has resulted in an unintended signal of discouragement to talented girls and women." The poor little dears so allegedly maligned were upset, and so Larry Summers went from treating women in the academy as intellectually curious, self-assured professionals to delicate victims whose fragile self-esteem he had inadvertently bruised.

When Summers's plea that his remarks had been misconstrued did little to quell the feminist-fueled controversy (Gloria Feldt, president of Planned Parenthood, piled on, seeing the episode as an example of our culture's deep bias against women), he announced the appointment of two faculty task forces on women and promised to create a senior administrative position to boost gender diversity. Like a docile graduate of a brutal reeducation regime, Dr. Summers declared, "I think what's important is that we move forward in strong and exciting ways."

Heather Mac Donald of the Manhattan Institute nailed the ensuing "Report of the Task Force on Women's Faculty" as "a peerless example of the destruction of higher learning by identity politics."[42]

The tribute to political correctness was a $50 million pledge over ten years to increase diversity at Harvard, and one of Summers's harshest critics, Professor Theda Skocpol, was named dean of the Graduate School of Arts and Sciences. The sociology and government professor is a victorious veteran of Harvard's diversity wars, having filed a grievance in 1980 claiming sex discrimination when she was denied tenure at the university. Mac Donald points out that "[G]iven that Harvard and its competitors across the country have already beaten the bushes for years for 'diversity' candidates, even $500 million would seem unlikely to produce any major change in Harvard's 'diversity' profile."[43] But, the contrition racket won a promotion for Professor Skocpol and a new top spot for a diversity czarina, "supported by a group of dedicated staff," as a senior vice provost.[44] There are well-paying jobs to be had when the patriarchy is had.

The Summers episode is a testament to the clout feminists enjoy in the academy and to the hostility of feminist *scientists* to academic inquiry. As Charles Murray explains, "If you were to query all the scholars who deal professionally with data about the cognitive repertories of men and women, all but a fringe would accept that the sexes are different, and that genes are clearly implicated."[45]

Dr. Nancy Hopkins is also a veteran of intimidation campaigns against universities. In 2001, *The New York Times* noted that the MIT professor "has become the emblem of the struggle by women for equal treatment in higher education." When Hopkins filed a complaint with MIT's president alleging discrimination against female faculty members, she was put in charge of the committee created to investigate her complaint. In March 1999, her committee produced *A Study on the Status of Women Faculty in Science at MIT*. The prestigious university confessed to "institutionalized" bias, and the report landed on the front page of *The New York Times*. Following his feminist reeducation, Robert J. Birgeneau, dean of the accused school at the time, said, "It wasn't gross discrimination, but what these women came to understand was that part of their marginalization was a series of minor insults."[46] The payoff was major.

The Ford Foundation gave MIT a million dollars to investigate and redress the alleged discrimination against women faculty members, and Nancy Hopkins got a salary hike, new grants, a spot on the National Academy of Science's Institute of Medicine, and an invitation to the White House.[47] Feminists like Professors Hopkins and Skocpol can typically count on enjoying kudos and promotions when intimidated officials surrender to their demands for "diversity."

Nine months later, the Independent Women's Forum (IWF) published a critique of the MIT study by Dr. Judith Kleinfeld that found methodological flaws and serious omissions in Hopkins's handiwork. Kleinfeld concluded, "The explanation for the sex disparity is the shortage of women in these scientific fields overall, not gender discrimination on the part of MIT."

The MIT study provided no objective evidence of bias, and no evidence documenting disparities in working conditions. It concluded that female faculty "proved to be underpaid," but acknowledged "primary salary data are confidential and were not provided to us." One committee member later stated, "I never felt marginalized," and the report admitted that younger women on the faculty "feel that men and women are treated equally."[48]

A 2001 report on MIT's biology department commissioned by the IWF did find a disparity between male and female professors. Male scientists published more often, were more frequently cited in scientific journals, and brought in more grant money.

Gender politics saw a great university adopt a phony gender equity, and in their demand for special treatment, feminists once again put professional women under suspicion that they owe their position to something other than merit. When she weighed in on the Summers dispute, Dr. Kleinfeld cited Johns Hopkins University's talent search, which has included over a million students since 1971. Students who score over 700 on the math SAT at age thirteen, before they've had advanced mathematical training, are included in the program. There are thirteen males who qualify for every female. She points out that the mathematically precocious girls typically have higher verbal abilities and broader interests than the boys. These differences can understandably lead to different career choices.[49]

Feminists like Carol Gilligan, Peggy Orenstein, Mary Pipher, Katherine Hanson, and Nancy Hopkins have been waging a destructive gender war in our schools and universities that has harmed girls, boys, and serious scholarship. For thirty years they have been working to wipe out sex differences like chalk from a blackboard. Their ideological theories demand equal outcomes rather than an opportunity for young men and women to pursue their own interests free of feminist engineering. Our children are neither little victims nor pint-size oppressors. They aren't pathological creatures in need of feminist therapies. Based on their education record, women bent on politicizing our schools and waging a war of the sexes in America's classrooms should be expelled from school.

5 | Spoil Sports— Boys Benched

The feminists' signature brew of dishonesty, intimidation, and hypocrisy has been the familiar recipe in the campaign they claim is designed to increase the number of women who engage in sports. Here again, the goal is not simply creating more opportunities for female athletes. In the name of leveling the playing field, these women are determined to tackle the male dominance in sports, which they see as a despised vestige of male privilege and prowess, and a precursor to male violence. Under Title IX of the Educational Amendments of 1972 aimed at prohibiting sex discrimination in education programs receiving federal funds, the goalpost has been moved: from increasing athletic opportunities for women to reducing the number of men playing sports to achieve parity between the sexes. And the quota has placed a premium on female athletes that disadvantages the great majority of women when they apply to universities.

Gender quotas for college athletes have been a triumph for the feminist movement. They meet a feminist ideological goal while extracting a heavy price from the despised sex. The government enforces equal outcomes under the guise of equal opportunity and openly discriminates against men. Thousands of slots for male athletes on intercollegiate teams have been eliminated over the past fifteen years, in the name of fairness.

ON THE OFFENSE AGAINST MEN'S SPORTS

Eleanor Smeal's Feminist Majority Foundation reveals the real target of the feminists' interest in sports "equality" when it explains, "By encouraging boys to become aggressive, violent athletes, and by encouraging girls to cheer for them, we perpetuate the cycle of male aggression and violence against women." Feminists believe today's running back is tomorrow's rapist.

The Super Bowl Sunday domestic-battery lie that feminists peddled in 1993 is a classic example of their determination to link male sports fans with violence against women. Prior to that year's game, women's groups announced that football's biggest day was "the biggest day of the year for violence against women," claiming that there were increases of up to 40 percent in pleas for help from victims on that dark day. Nancy Isaac, a domestic violence expert at Harvard School of Public Health, announced, "It's a day for men to revel in their maleness and unfortunately, for a lot of men that includes being violent toward women if they want to." Journalists credulously bought the story, and NBC cautioned its male viewers to remain calm. The claim was wholly bogus.[1] A *Washington Post* reporter investigated the charge and concluded, "Despite their dramatic claims, none of the activists appears to have any evidence that a link actually exists between football and wife-beating. Yet the concept has gained such credence that their campaign has rolled on anyway, unabated."[2]

The number of female athletes has increased dramatically since the early seventies, when young women weren't encouraged to play competitive sports and only three hundred thousand high school girls did. Unfortunately, in my all-girls high school good grooming trumped the importance of an outside shot in gym class. Neatly pressed gym uniforms were the priority for our gym teacher, who elegantly presided over class in stockings and heels. Apparently, ironing was supposed to contribute to our physical fitness. One of my sisters, a promising competitive swimmer, exited the pool and dried off for good when my mother observed that the large shoulders she risked developing would look terrible in evening clothes. While she remains perfectly happy with her choice, no doubt other young women would have benefited had they been encouraged to stay in the pool.

Today, 2.4 million high school girls enjoy the benefits of competitive sports. However, in both high school and college, the proportion of female students playing sports has, after an initial surge, leveled off to less than 40 percent. At the college level, women make up about 57 percent of enrollment nationwide (although only 48 percent of full-time undergraduate students, presumably those who have the time be playing sports) and 41 percent of college athletes. A sensible person might conclude that this reflects women's natural inclination to be less interested in sports. A nonsensible person would bitterly complain even when girls are participating at a much higher rate than the national average. Here again, feminists ignore women's individual preferences and vehemently refuse to recognize obvious group differences between men and women. The National Women's Law Center warned Massachusetts officials in 2004 that they had better get busy enforcing "gender equity" because the 50 percent of girls statewide playing on one or more sports teams (versus 40 percent nationally) compares unfavorably with the 58 percent of high school boys on teams.

Men are demonstrably more interested in playing and watching sports than women. Men make up 60 percent of the TV audience for the women's NCAA basketball finals. A study of Division I-A schools found that 70 percent of men, but only 45 percent of women, engaged in intramural sports, the voluntary and open teams that can accurately gauge students' interests.[3] An analysis conducted by the College Board found that twice as many men as women said they wanted to play sports in college.[4] Studies show that girls in high school are a large majority in extracurricular activities like band and debate clubs and dominate in student government, journalism, and service clubs. They are clearly joiners. But boys make up a large majority of sports participants. Youth sports leagues independent of schools indicate the same natural discrepancy. About 2.4 million children, almost all of them boys, play Little League baseball. Little League softball has only 384,000 players, almost all of them girls.

Feminists insist that girls' comparative lack of interest in athletics is the result of social conditioning to avoid traditionally male activities. They ignore high school girls' current leadership in other traditionally male interests like journalism, debate, and student government. The stubborn, undeniable fact that women are typically less interested in playing sports than men frustrates the feminist project to see equal numbers of men and women on the courts and in the bleachers.

Owing to the legitimate differences between the sexes and among women, feminists have been unable to boost the number of women interested in suiting up to match the number of men anxious to engage in sports. Their remedy is to eliminate opportunities

for men so they are unable to demonstrate their greater, natural interest in sports. The result is that men's participation in sports is
capped at the level of women's interest. The celebration of the number of American women in the quest for gold at the 2004 Athens
Olympics is a classic example of feminists' scoring points at the expense of men in their drive to ensure equal outcomes despite obvious sex differences.

"As the result of years of emphasis on gender equity," *The Washington Post* reported, "for the first time, the U.S. Olympic team that
will compete at the Summer Games in Athens this August will have
nearly equal numbers of men and women."[5] The welcome news was
that the 263 women on the U.S. team represented more than 48
percent of the roster. Before the champagne corks pop, it should be
noted that the team roster was so pleasingly balanced because 56
fewer American men were on the 2004 team than fours years earlier.
In fact, the number of women on the roster had *decreased* since 2000.
There were 264 women on the team in 2000. What exactly is being
celebrated? Fewer American men were given a shot at going for the
gold.

The current enforcement of Title IX dictates a strict gender balance regardless of whether the result is an increase in opportunities
for women. It wasn't supposed to be this way. Title IX was enacted
as part of the Education Amendments of 1972. Congress was particularly concerned that women were being discriminated against in
college admissions. It simply says, "No person in the United States
shall, on the basis of sex, be excluded from participation in, be denied the benefits of, or be subjected to discrimination under any education program or activity receiving federal financial assistance."
At the time, then Senator Birch Bayh (D–IN), one of the law's chief
sponsors, explained that gender quotas were "exactly what this
amendment intends to prohibit. . . . The amendment does not con-

tain, nor does the Senator from Indiana feel it should contain, a quota which says there has to be a 50–50 ratio to meet the test." For good measure, an amendment to Title IX specifically prohibited granting "preferential or disparate treatment to the members of one sex on account of an imbalance."

Today, there is an imbalance on America's campuses—in favor of women. Women make up 57 percent of undergraduates and earn a majority of all master's degrees. But feminists aren't content with this remarkable educational success, because female students aren't playing sports to the same extent as men.

In the name of "equal participation," according to the NCAA, 200 men's teams, and over 20,000 male slots on team rosters, were eliminated between 1992 and 1997. During the same time, the number of female athletes increased by 5,800. Nearly four men were dropped from teams for each woman who joined a roster. Title IX has been four times more effective in eliminating male athletes than in developing female athletes. The NCAA reports that there are now more women's teams than men's among its members, but male rosters remain larger, and so, as one university coach puts it, the "carnage" afflicting men's sports continues. When they contemplate this carnage, feminists want to see Title IX's enforcement strengthened. "Its biggest problem is that it hasn't been enforced strongly enough to get women's athletics into a position of equality," according to Marcia Greenberger, co-president of the National Women's Law Center. "It's been too moderate," she declared in 2001.

By 1999, an estimated 354 men's teams had been axed, and over twenty thousand young men were no longer able to play intercollegiate sports. UCLA's men's swimming team, which had produced some of our most successful Olympic competitors, was shut down. The University of Miami, where four-time gold medalist Greg Louganis trained, axed its men's crew, swimming, and diving teams.

In the late nineties, sixteen Division I schools dropped their men's swim teams and more than sixty schools eliminated men's track programs. The California State University system signed a consent decree with NOW in 1993. The female head coach of softball at California State University at Northridge explained that the clear difference in interest was evident by men's willingness to remain on team rosters even if they didn't get to play, while women quit teams if they didn't get to take to the field. It didn't matter. By 1997, the men's baseball, soccer, volleyball, and swimming teams were eliminated to meet NOW's demands.

In 1972, there were 777 college wrestling programs; there were only 315 by 1996 despite enormous interest at the high school level. Florida has 253 high-school wrestling programs with over six thousand participants, but no college teams at any level. The majority of male athletes who lost slots were nonscholarship students who were dropped because male rosters had to be reduced. Their elimination didn't create any new opportunities for women. When Princeton University dropped its men's wrestling team to meet the proportionality test, an alumni group offered to raise the $2 million necessary to reconstitute the team. But Princeton couldn't accept the private money unless they created some new sports program for women to keep team rosters in balance. There is no men's wrestling at Princeton any longer.

Former Senator Bayh has lately explained, "That was not the purpose of Title IX. And that has been a very unfortunate aspect of this. The idea of Title IX was not to give fewer opportunities to men; it was to make more opportunities for women."

STRICT QUOTAS BENCH BOYS

Senator Bayh and his colleagues didn't appreciate that feminists had a wholly different idea. Feminist groups have used intimidation and litigation to transform a law intended to eliminate discrimination against women into a law demanding discrimination against men. When then Congressman Charles Canady of Florida attempted to remind his colleagues about the clear words of Title IX prohibiting preferential treatment for either sex, California Congresswoman Maxine Waters interrupted his reading of the statute with a delighted cackle, "It's the biggest quota you've ever seen. It is 50–50. It is a quota—big round quota." Give the left-wing lawmaker an A for honesty. Her feminist sisters at the Women's Sports Foundation dishonestly claim no quotas are at work, while fighting to make sure they are strictly enforced.

The Women's Sports Foundation, NOW, the National Coalition for Woman and Girls, the National Women's Law Center, and the Feminist Majority Foundation have lobbied compliant liberal bureaucrats at the Department of Education and launched aggressive lawsuits to enforce a strict 50–50 gender quota in collegiate sports. Donna Lopiano, executive director of the Women's Sports Foundation, fessed up to the agenda in 1992 when she told reporters that her intent was to "break the bank" by forcing schools to spend such huge sums to meet gender quotas that the whole, hated male-dominated structure of college sports would collapse and be replaced by "gender equity."[6]

Although feminists solely credit Title IX with increasing the number of female students playing sports, the numbers were on the rise before the law was passed as women were increasing their participation in athletics along with other nontraditional activities. Not for the first time, a natural evolution in social expectations was occurring that feminists were quick to attribute to their activism.

As Jessica Gavora points out in her well-researched and well-argued book *Tilting the Playing Field: Schools, Sports, Sex and Title IX*, the NCAA reports that the number of women playing intercollegiate sports doubled in the five years before Title IX. Gavora comes to her compelling critique as a former athlete, who as one of nine children grew up challenging her brothers in one-on-one games under the family's basketball hoop in Fairbanks, Alaska. Tall and lithe, she looks like a woman who once played basketball, as she says, "devotedly, fanatically." She credits athletics with providing crucial lessons about success and failure, physical fitness, and teamwork. She needs no convincing about the benefits sports provide young women, but she recalls growing up with "an almost limitless opportunity" and wants her own young daughter to inherit the same ability to freely pursue her own interests and ambitions. Gender feminists will never convince her that women are passive victims of a controlling patriarchy or that young men should be denied opportunities in an ideological pursuit of equal outcomes.

Gavora recounts a telling story about the treatment critics can expect when they "betray their sex" and dissent from feminist orthodoxy to question the relevancy of the modern women's movement to the majority of American women. Following the taping of a combative but civil debate with a leader of the pro-quota women's movement, the veteran feminist sternly lectured her, "Jessica, I'm going to say something to you that someone should have said a long time ago. You don't have any idea of the damage you're doing to women. Someday I hope you'll understand the irresponsibility of the things you're saying." Gavora responded, "If you have a quarrel with the points I made and the facts I presented, why didn't you make it when the cameras were rolling, instead of trying to intimidate me in the parking lot?" There is no "choice" when it comes to accepting the monolithic views of gender feminists. Accomplished, self-assured, independent-minded women like Jessica Gavora threaten the feminist hegemony.

In questioning the alleged importance of Title IX in boosting women's involvement in sports, Gavora points out that the percentage of female athletes was 5.5 percent of women collegians in 1986.

The number of female student-athletes has slowly increased since then, as the number of women undergraduates has also increased. Only recently has the percentage of women athletes (157,000) met the 1986 high-water mark of 5.5 percent of all female full-time undergraduates.

Preoccupied with their futile attempt to win enough states' approval of the Equal Rights Amendment, feminists didn't much bother with Title IX for years after its passage. When the ERA flopped, they turned their attention to it. In 1979, the feminists' sports groups pressured the Department of Education's Office of Civil Rights (OCR) to issue a Policy Interpretation that would be used to determine if a college's athletics program was in compliance with Title IX. The directive, never approved by Congress, laid out three ways a school could comply with the law's mandate that its sports programs not discriminate against women.

Schools would be in compliance if: 1) the ratio of male and female athletes is "substantially proportionate" to the ratio of male and female students; or 2) it could be demonstrated that there was a history of expanding opportunities for athletes of the underrepresented sex; or 3) it could be shown that the "athletic interests and abilities" of the underrepresented sex had been fully accommodated.

In the following years, college athletic programs were considered in compliance with the statute if the school had a history of expanding athletic opportunities for women, or could demonstrate that the interest in sports by women on its campus was being accommodated. There were only three formal Title IX reviews of college athletic programs during the 1980s. But then along came Norma.

Norma V. Cantú became President Bill Clinton's assistant secretary for civil rights at the Department of Education in 1993. Before heading to Washington to head up the OCR, Cantú had been a regional counsel for the Mexican American Legal Defense and Education Fund (MALDEF). For ten years, she had served as the national director of the MALDEF Education Litigation and Advocacy Project. A litigious fox was in charge of the collegiate chicken coops. The feminist crusader had a $66 million annual budget and seven hundred employees to enforce civil rights laws, covering race, sex, and disabilities, as she saw fit. A stern letter from her office to a school signaled expensive legal trouble ahead. She was known to warn schools about the biggest weapon in her enforcement arsenal—she could seek to cut off all federal funds, including student aid and big research grants.

Despite her soothing words about "collaboration and partnership" with schools to enforce Title IX, Cantú made it clear that only the strict proportionality test would keep colleges out of trouble with her office. By 1995, Cantú was openly calling the 50–50 proportionality test the "safe haven" for schools wishing to avoid the threat of an OCR inquiry or lawsuit.

Meanwhile, feminists had gone to court in the hope of winning a ruling to enforce the proportionality test. Über-progressive Brown University was an early enthusiastic supporter of athletic opportunities for women. In 1991, budget-cutting at the university led to the elimination of two women's teams and two men's teams, affecting thirty-seven men and twenty-three women. Kathryn Reith, a Brown graduate and director of advocacy at the Women's Sports Foundation, had found the plaintiffs she had been looking for in Brown's disgruntled female gymnasts. A class-action suit was filed in 1992. It mattered not that Brown had almost twice as many women's sports teams as other Division I schools, and that women's teams outnumbered men's on campus. There was no inequality in sports scholarships because neither men nor women received athletic aid. At the time of the lawsuit, there were 93 unfilled slots on women's varsity teams. Surveys of high school students interested in attending Brown indicated that 60 percent of men and 40 percent of women intended to play sports on campus. The only thing that mattered was that 51 percent of Brown's students were female and only 38 percent of its athletes were women.

Brown argued that it provided athletic opportunities sufficient to meet the interest and abilities of its female students, but the court ruled that under Title IX schools must structure teams so the ratio of male to female athletes matches the ratio in the student body. Brown was told to fund any sport women might want to play, regardless of cost, or eliminate 213 slots for men. Despite the unambiguous words of Title IX, the federal court created a specific preference for women by adopting Donna Lopiano's (a star witness for the plaintiffs) "field of dreams" argument that if you build it women will come. Brown was told to presume that "women, given the opportunity, will naturally participate in athletics in numbers equal to men."

The feminist "field of dreams" theory is impossible to square with facts on the playing fields. Men outnumbered women eight to one in Brown's intramural program, which had no limits on participation. And by 1997, Brown's seventeen women's sports teams all had openings on their rosters, while the sixteen men's teams all had long waiting lists.

The National Women's Law Center celebrated the twenty-fifth anniversary of Title IX by filing complaints with their friend Norma against twenty-five other universities whose athletic teams don't have the same male-female ratios as their student bodies. Only athletics programs are subject to strict sex quotas. Dance programs can be 90 percent female, and nursing or early-education degrees can be awarded to a disproportionate number of women. Colleges have reacted to the threat of lawsuits over the uneven gender balance in their sports programs by aggressively recruiting women who express an interest in playing varsity sports. This preference in admissions for female athletes clearly disadvantages the majority of young women, who don't choose to be active in athletics.

I have no beef with the Title IX advocates' claim that women can benefit from playing sports. Unlike them, I agree with Jessica Gavora when she recognizes that our sons and brothers also benefit from the physical conditioning, teamwork, and sense of achievement they gain by taking part in athletic competitions. Schools actively recruit athletes of both sexes because they recognize that students have much to gain from competitive sports, and universities benefit by fielding successful teams.

GIRLS SHOULD CRY FOUL

Universities hope for a mix among their student bodies that reflects different interests and talents. But the federal government has put a premium on a specific interest and talent. Gavora summarizes the results of a comprehensive study about athletic preferences that shatters the myth that women generally benefit from the current enforcement of Title IX.

In *The Game of Life: College Sports and Educational Values*, James Shulman and William Bowen examine data on ninety thousand students who attended thirty selective universities. The authors conclude that female athletes are the most preferred of all students whose admissions are the result of affirmative action. In 1999, at a "representative" nonscholarship school, a female minority had a 20 percent admissions advantage, the daughter of an alumnus had a 24 percent advantage, while a female athlete had a 53 percent advantage. That is, Gavora writes, "a female athlete had a 53 percent better chance of being admitted than a non-athlete with the same SAT score."[7] A female college applicant interested in drama or chemistry or debate who is rejected by a prestigious school in favor of a female candidate who plans on playing varsity field hockey can thank Title IX.

Women athletes on campus are achieving equality with their male counterparts by one measure. Shulman and Bowen report that female athletes now lag academically behind female nonathletes, just as there is a gap in academic achievement between male athletes and male nonathletes. In 1976, female athletes were less likely than other female students to bring up the bottom of the class at graduation. By 1989, 39 percent of female athletes graduated in the bottom third of their class, in contrast with 29 percent of other female students.

If women's comparative lack of interest in athletics is a legacy of male oppression and previous discrimination, it would be logical to assume that women at women's colleges who never had to share facilities or funds with men would represent their sex's unadulterated interest in sports. And today, the largely liberal women at liberal all-women's colleges are probably among the most aggressive women on the planet. But surveys conducted by the Independent Women's Forum indicate that on average only about 15 percent of women at schools like Smith, Wellesley, and Bryn Mawr play sports.

Although male coaches and administrators and parents of boys shut out of sports have generally meekly complied with the quota regime, wrestling coaches have gone to the mat over the enforced ratios that have decimated their sport. In 2004, a federal court dismissed a suit alleging reverse discrimination against male athletes brought by the National Wrestling Coaches Association on the grounds that the association wasn't the object of Title IX's policy. But individual male athletes have been no more successful in challenging Title IX's sex quotas.

The wrestling coaches did get the attention of Education Secretary Rod Paige, who appointed the Commission on Opportunity in Athletics to consider possible reforms to the enforcement of Title IX. In the mistaken belief that reasonable people could take a reasonable look at the obviously unfair results of Cantú-style Title IX enforcement, some feminists were appointed to the blue ribbon panel. Julie Foudy and Donna de Varona, president and past president of the Women's Sports Foundation, were appointed to the commission. They adopted the feminist tactic of arguing that quotas don't exist while fighting to preserve their strict enforcement.

In early 2003 the commission delivered its report, and within hours of receiving it, Secretary Paige announced that he would ignore a third of its recommendations and only consider its unanimous suggestions. Although five of the seven female members of the commission, including a coach, an athletic director, and a WNBA all-star, supported sensible reforms to Title IX, Paige's insistence on unanimity granted the feminist commissioners a veto over the panel's conclusions. Secretary Paige joined a long list of public officials to hear the shrill demands of feminists and mistake them for the legitimate aspirations of American women.

Foudy and de Varona, former Olympic medalists in soccer and swimming, cried foul over the majority conclusions of the commission. They objected to the recommendation that schools not count walk-ons, who are predominantly male, when team rosters are considered for compliance with Title IX and to the recommendation that nontraditional students, typically older women, not be included in enrollment calculations.

Even the vague unanimous conclusions (noting that cutting men's teams to comply with Title IX is disfavored and suggesting the Department of Education should explore other ways to demonstrate "equity") were loudly condemned by feminist groups. Actresses Geena Davis and Holly Hunter vowed to lead a campaign to get the entire report shelved.

In March 2005, the Cantú-less, post-Paige Department of Education issued a "clarification" to Title IX enforcement that will allow schools to determine students' interest in sports by conducting a survey. The evidence of students' relative interest may help schools that lack a 50–50 balance in teams show that disinclination rather than discrimination is at play when the playing fields aren't in perfect balance. No doubt in fear that the interest surveys will identify a lack of interest on the part of many women students, feminists howled in response to this commonsense reform.

On the thirty-third anniversary of Title IX in June 2005, House minority leader Nancy Pelosi announced that 140 of her fellow Democrats had written President Bush to demand that he withdraw the Education Department's clarification. Senator Hillary Clinton declared, "There is some short-sighted thinking going on in this administration. There really isn't any good reason [for us to] have to stand up for girls to have equal access to sports." In the classic deception of such women, the strict proportionality they demand is sold as "equal access."

Marcia Greenberger of the National Women's Law Center sees the guidelines as "an underhanded way to weaken Title IX and make it easy for schools that aren't interested in providing equal opportunity for women to skirt [sic] the law."[8] The gender warriors are clearly prepared to ignore what the surveys reveal. "Surveys are likely to reflect past discrimination," Neena Chaudhry of Greenberger's law center argued.[9]

There is no evidence that women's lagging interest in playing sports is the result of sex discrimination, but a feminist ideology that denies sex differences will charge discrimination wherever group differences are found. In the area of college sports, feminists have succeeded in pressuring the government to use Title IX, an antidiscrimination statute, to enforce a strict quota system that discriminates against young men. And the majority of young women, who don't play sports, now face an uneven playing field when they compete against a female athlete in seeking college admission.

In 2002, when Bowling Green State University announced the elimination of men's tennis, track, swimming, and diving programs, having already cut men's wrestling and lacrosse, Debra Downing and Alice Springer fought to save their sons' teams because, according to Springer, they are not the kind of women prone to "rolling over."[10] If more mothers of boys took on Hillary Clinton, Nancy Pelosi, Marcia Greenberger, and the other women who have caused so many of their sons to lose out on playing the sports they love, there would be a genuinely level playing field.

FEMINISTS MISS THE CUT AT THE MASTERS

While Secretary Paige was hoisting a white flag in response to incoming feminist fire, another target of the feminists' wrath was successfully standing his ground. The contrast is instructive. When feminists' bluff is called, it becomes clear that they don't speak for the "millions" of women they claim to represent and that they lack widespread support for an ideological agenda that pits men against women.

William "Hootie" Johnson refused to appease feminists when the Augusta National Golf Club, home to the Masters Tournament, became a target for one of their campaigns of intimidation. Martha Burk was head of the National Council of Women's Organizations (NCWO), an umbrella group of about 100 feminist outfits, who claims to represent a big slice of American women. In April 2002, Burk read in USA Today that the Augusta National Golf Club in Georgia had not had a woman member in its seventy years. Always vigilant on the gender police patrol, she fired off a letter to Hootie Johnson, the club's chairman, demanding that the club open its membership to women. She no doubt then turned her attention to haranguing some other poor soul for offending her sisters' sensibilities, but this time she had picked on the wrong guy. A few months later, she got a response in the form of a press release from the delightfully defiant, colorful seventy-two-year-old Johnson.

"Our members are people who enjoy each other's company and the game of golf," he said. They "will not be bullied, threatened or intimidated. . . . There may well come a day when women will be invited to join our membership, but that timetable will be ours and not at the point of a bayonet." He told Burk, "I have found your letter's several references to discrimination, allusions to the sponsors and your setting of deadlines to be both offensive and coercive."

Hootie Johnson was an early champion of desegregation and the first white Southerner to serve on the Urban League's board of directors, but Burk and her feminist allies would attempt to liken him to a white supremacist resisting integration when the battle was joined over his refusal to knuckle under to their demands. When he told *The New York Times*, "We hold dear our traditions and our constitutional right to choose," he showed he was good on offense and was maybe even enjoying the face-off with feminists. "Constitutional right to choose"? Take that, Martha.

Johnson argued that as a private club, Augusta National had the right to determine who could join. Augusta National, with its 280 members, had no policy prohibiting female members, but no women had ever been invited to join, although they were allowed to play the course as guests. Burk claimed that the club is open to the public because it hosts the prestigious Masters Tournament, so it couldn't discriminate against women. Going for his third straight championship in 2003, Tiger Woods agreed that a private club should be able to invite the golfers it wanted, although he would welcome a change in Augusta's policy. "If others had taken that view, he'd be a caddie at Augusta," Burk declared.[11]

She pressured the tournament's corporate sponsors. Johnson dropped corporate sponsorship from the next tournament. To the delight of its fans, the tournament was carried on TV with no commercials in 2003 and 2004.

Burk's campaign and protests fizzled, despite receiving the lavish press attention feminists can typically count on. *USA Today* assigned twenty-three reporters to the showdown; *The Atlanta Journal-Constitution* had twenty covering the dispute. Under former executive editor Howell Raines, *The New York Times* treated the feminist assault on the Augusta National as though it were the most consequential story of the year. It ran dozens of stories critical of Johnson, and reporters filed sometimes daily dispatches on the dispute as though reporting on the progress of a high-stakes shooting war.

Ultimately, Burk was firing blanks. This antiwar activist even exploited American military women dying in Iraq to argue that Augusta National should bend to her will. "It's appalling that the women who are willing to lay down their lives for democratic ideals should be shut out of this club," she exclaimed.[12] A poll commissioned by the club found a large majority of men and women thought private clubs should have the right to define their membership by gender. When Martha Burk held a protest outside the Masters tournament in 2003, the mere forty protesters who joined her were easily outnumbered by the police and reporters present. George Vecsey, one of her cheerleaders at *The New York Times*, gamely tried to save face. He wrote, "Numbers were never the goal. Burk got people talking. She got under their skin."[13]

The AP reported that one year after Martha Burk was run ragged with hundreds of media interviews, she "has been in the news only twice this year" and "the incendiary issue that once threatened to become an inferno has all but fizzled."[14]

By 2005, Burk had launched a shakedown operation against corporate America. Her outfit began soliciting employee plaintiffs for class action lawsuits against companies that sponsored the Masters Tournament because they "are associating themselves with a venue that openly and proudly discriminates against women, which sends a debilitating message to female employees." And she recruited her congressional allies to prohibit the deduction of expenses for "discriminatory clubs" on corporate tax returns.[15] Burk has fingered for her hall-of-shame treatment top executives at companies who belong to Augusta, including American Express, Citigroup, and Morgan Stanley. What should deeply shame these corporations is that they have all been generous supporters of feminist groups that belong to Burk's National Council.[16] In November 2005, Burk stepped aside as head of the NCWO to concentrate on intimidating American businesses full-time through the feminist group's "Corporate Accountability Project."

6 | G.I. Janes

The military came under attack because an assault on an occupation defined by the masculine qualities it demands would satisfy the fundamental feminist enterprise of denying any consequential differences between the sexes. Throughout recorded history, men have fought their nations' wars. (Only the French looked to a teenage girl to lead them in battle.) Feminists knew that winning the "right" for women to kill and be killed beside men would be a triumph over far more than women's limited career options. It would be a successful challenge to masculinity and the male imperative to protect the weaker sex. The aim is to deny that a soldier's attributes of physical courage, aggression, and risk-taking are quintessential male traits.

Thousands of women serve proudly in uniform, doing all that the military asks of them. But their admirable service should be in noncombat positions, thereby freeing men to be on the front lines. In the name of a phony equality, the military shouldn't ask them to serve where they don't have an equal chance to survive.

In a celebratory story featured on its Web site, the U.S. Army patted itself on the back for giving Army Reserve Sergeant Julia Fadell the opportunity to drive a forty-ton heavy equipment transporter throughout Iraq rather than be stuck in a dreaded "routine job." By October 2003, Sergeant Fadell had been fired on and separated from the unit's convoy at night in Baghdad, but was extending for another year's duty in Operation Iraqi Freedom. "What I'm doing is important," declared the forty-one-year-old mother of six children who range in age from nine to twenty-two. In keeping with the apparent family tradition of women doing men's dangerous work, her eldest daughter, an Air Force reservist, had recently served in Baghdad. Mother and daughter are a tribute to the feminists who have waged a relentless campaign against the quintessentially male obligation to fight our nation's wars. Feminist ideology has won when it doesn't matter which sex does the mothering or the soldiering.

WOMEN IN THE LINE OF FIRE

The 18,000 military women serving in Iraq and Afghanistan are in greater danger than during any previous deployment. More have been killed by hostile fire than in any engagement since women were integrated into the armed forces in 1948. By the end of 2004, more than 230 women serving in Iraq and Afghanistan had been awarded the Purple Heart for wounds inflicted by the enemy. By June 2005, 37 female soldiers had been killed in Iraq, and 285 had been wounded.

During the Vietnam War, when it was understood that brutal combat was what the military did for a living, women made up about 1 percent of U.S. troops. In Vietnam, only eight of the more than 58,000 Americans killed were women, all unarmed nurses. The number of women on active duty in the all-volunteer force, helped along by gender "goals" in recruiting, gradually increased during the relative peace of the past thirty years. Women now make up 6 percent of the Marine Corps, about 15 percent of the Navy and Army, and over 19 percent of the Air Force. The recruiting quotas that put a premium on getting young women to sign up are costly. Before their first three years in uniform are completed, almost 47 percent of enlisted women have left the service, compared with about 28 percent of males.[1]

The stubborn conviction that there is nothing distinct about the military's call to kill and be killed, that women serving in combat is merely an extension of women working outside the home, was expressed by a female Marine officer in her e-mail to the media from Iraq. "Gender has no relevance in the Marine Corps today," she wrote. "The ideal of equality is not just about the right to vote or work. This notion that women are somehow not able to perform their jobs in the military in a combat environment flies in the face of everything we say we value in the USA."[2]

The 213,059 women on active duty include over 24,000 single mothers, and there are 29,000 married women with children on active duty in the Army alone. Women in the military are twice as likely to be single parents as their male comrades. And while female soldiers are less likely to be married than male soldiers, women in uniform who are married are more likely to have children.

The first female casualty in Iraq was Army Private First Class Lori Piestewa, a twenty-four-year-old supply clerk and single mother of a four-year-old son and three-year-old daughter. In previous conflicts, Lori Piestewa and her best friend, nineteen-year-old Jessica Lynch, would not have been surrounded by the enemy in that ambushed convoy. Women who volunteered to serve in the military were protected from being involuntarily assigned perilously close to combat. But Bill Clinton's Pentagon dared not risk frustrating feminists like Congresswoman Pat Schroeder, who began her career as an antiwar activist and ended it as an enemy general in the Pentagon's gender war, which is the only war she has ever been interested in winning. The Pentagon's "Risk Rule," which prohibited assigning women to units that posed a risk of attack or capture, was repealed by Defense Secretary Les Aspin in 1994.

When the number of women who died in Iraq reached two dozen, sixteen as the result of enemy action, feminists welcomed the gruesome milestone. Retired Air Force brigadier general Wilma L. Vaught explained, "There's been an acceptance of the fact that women . . . are in harm's way and they are being killed. That is defining to me."[3] A woman being brutally killed alongside men is a long-awaited feminist dream of equality. Gloria Feldt, president of Planned Parenthood, wants to see even more casualties, with more abortions added to the body count. She cites women on the front lines in Iraq as a justification for performing abortions in military hospitals overseas. "The women who have been deployed to Iraq to fight our war for us are not trusted by our government to make their own childbearing choices," she proclaimed. The abuse and deaths of teenage girls and young single mothers are exploited to advance the feminist agenda of androgyny and abortion.

Vaught is one of the aging feminists who retired from the military with a big chip on their shoulder boards, a careerist agenda, and a resolve to redress their past grievances by waging war on the military's combat exemption for women. Their allies include congresswomen; civilian appointees at the Pentagon, Democratic and Republican alike; feminist academics; and past members of the Pentagon's feminist lobby, the (now reformed) Defense Advisory Committee on Women in the Services (DACOWITS). The military provided a perfect petri dish for their experiments in social engineering because it's a coercive environment where people can be counted on to follow orders, however destructive.

It is estimated that repealing the Risk Rule opened 80 percent of all military jobs to women. Recruiters acknowledged that there was no special effort to inform female recruits that there had been a change in assignment policies that would expose them to risk of combat or capture. The only positions that remain closed to women in the modern military are infantry and Special Forces units and submarines. While feminists profess to be advancing career opportunities for women in uniform by fighting for their equal right to die on the battlefield, a 1998 General Accounting Office report cited a Rand study that found only 10 percent of female privates and corporals agreed that "women should be treated exactly like men and serve in combat arms just like men."

Army Research Institute surveys since 1993 repeatedly found that 85 to 90 percent of female enlisted soldiers were opposed to being assigned combat roles on the same involuntary basis as male soldiers. The Army stopped asking women soldiers their opinion about serving in combat in 2001.

The three unfortunate young women who were captured by the enemy in the first days of the war in Iraq were accorded feminist icon status by liberals who welcomed the opportunity for someone else's daughter to face abuse or summary execution right alongside the guys. In what passes as logic for feminists, who demand they be treated as rational thinkers, Rosemary Mariner, one of the Navy's first female pilots, figures what's the big deal about women dying in combat; female civilians can be killed by terrorists. She blithely explained, "And in no small way, 9/11 points out that noncombatants in office buildings can get killed in a terrorist attack. It's no surprise to anyone that members of a combat service support unit can find themselves ambushed in Iraq. It shows how far the public has come."[4] But the female soldiers' families did express surprise that their threatened loved ones were so vulnerable.

Army Specialist Shoshana Johnson's older sister explained that the war's first female POW had joined the Army to train as a chef and never expected to be in such danger. "It never even crossed our mind that she'd be right up in the front lines. When it happened, we thought it [couldn't be] her."[5] Her aunt, an Army veteran from the days when female soldiers served in relative safety behind the front lines, declared, "She shouldn't be facing this. She was supposed to cook for the troops. This is so awful." Carolyn Becraft, an assistant secretary of the Navy in the Clinton administration, was unmoved by the unwitting fate of the single mother of a two-year-old daughter. "This is their job. These are the conditions of their employment," she told *The Washington Post*.[6]

Specialist Johnson and Private Lynch were rescued. Private First Class Lori Piestewa was not. Her "conditions of employment" were vividly depicted when, on December 30, 2003, NBC aired footage of Jessica Lynch and Lori Piestewa in custody following the ambush of the 507th maintenance company the previous March. Both bandaged young women appeared seriously hurt, with Lynch apparently unconscious and Piestewa, who died shortly afterward, grimacing in pain when her battered face was roughly turned for the camera. Her body was found in a shallow grave on the night Jessica Lynch was rescued. "She felt . . . she wasn't going to be anywhere near any type of dangerous situation," her brother told *USA Today*. Young Lori Piestewa was unaware that feminists like Wilma Vaught, Rosemary Mariner, and Carolyn Becraft had fought for years to put other people's sisters in harm's way.

As disclosed in her book about her ordeal, Jessica Lynch's "conditions of employment" included being raped by her captors. Lynch was delivered to a military hospital three hours after the ambush. According to *I Am a Soldier, Too*, "Her right arm was shattered between her shoulder and her elbow, and the compound fracture shoved slivers of bone through muscles, nerves and skin, leaving her right hand all but useless. Her spine was fractured in two places, causing nerve damage that left her unable to control her kidneys or bowels. Her right foot was crushed. Her left leg had broken into pieces above and below the knee . . . and left her without feeling in that limb." Her medical records don't indicate whether she was sexually assaulted before or after sustaining her grave injuries. *Newsweek* reported, "U.S. military intelligence officers believe Lynch's injuries were inflicted after she and other survivors surrendered." Three sources claimed she was standing, with minor injuries, when she surrendered. An Iraqi surgeon explained, "Her injuries appeared to have been inflicted by a severe beating, probably with rifle butts."[7]

The media's celebratory coverage of the teenager's rescue delicately avoided what she might have endured. When an Iraqi source gave a tip about Lynch's plight to an NBC reporter, he recounted that she had been tortured. The *New York Post* reported the tip, leaving out any reference to torture. Snapshots of sanitized yellow-ribbon moments reassure the public—and hide the reality of violence against America's daughters.

Good men protect and defend women in the face of a physical threat. If men in uniform are going to be expected to be sex blind when it comes to protecting their comrades, American mothers will have to get to work instructing their sons that it's okay to hit girls. Women have no "right" to serve in combat if their presence puts the men they serve with in jeopardy because these decent men are determined to protect the weaker sex. Instructors at the military's school for pilots saw that male students reacted more negatively to the simulated torture of female trainees and concluded that the men would have to be trained to inure themselves to the plight of women in pain.[8]

Feminists recognize the vulnerability of women when they are concerned with the plight of women who are victims of domestic abuse. They have no programs to reduce the level of violence between male roommates. Their position on integrating combat ranks puts them in the position of saying that violence against women is a terrible thing unless it is at the hands of the enemy, in which case it's a welcome tribute to women's equality.

WARTIME PROPAGANDA

Scores of men have received top awards for extraordinary heroism in battle during Operation Iraqi Freedom, but one of the rare front-page stories about a heroic soldier in a major newspaper was *The Washington Post's* April 3, 2003, account of Private Jessica Lynch firing away at the enemy "even after she sustained multiple gunshot wounds." The story, SHE WAS FIGHTING TO THE DEATH; DETAILS EMERGING OF W.VA. SOLDIER'S CAPTURE AND RESCUE, was picked up around the world—and was wholly false. Feminist commentators used the dramatic account to argue that direct combat positions should be open to women because Lynch had shown that "women can be as fierce as men."[9] Private Lynch later explained that she never fired a shot because her gun was jammed. *The Washington Post's* ombudsman questioned the initial story about two weeks after it appeared, but as he noted himself, "This was the single most memorable story of the war, and it had a unique propaganda value. It was false, but it didn't get knocked down until it didn't matter quite so much."

Minimizing the feats of men and exaggerating those of women is a familiar feminist tactic to promote their woman-as-warrior myth. Before there was Private Jessica Lynch there was Captain Linda Bray. Anxious to preempt any debate about the integration of women into combat, before feminists declared that Operation Iraqi Freedom has settled the case, they attempted to use Operation Just

Cause in Panama to put all questions to rest. Roughly seven hundred women were deployed to Panama in the eighteen thousand–strong invasion force, and a handful, although barred from serving in combat positions, were fired on when ferrying troops as either truck drivers or pilots. In 1990, Ellen Goodman wrote, "In word and deed, the military women in Panama have dispelled the favorite notions of sexists and many feminists alike that women are either intrinsically weaker or more peace-loving."[10] She cited the example of Captain Linda Bray and alleged that her "war heroine" story was rescripted because it was "too hot to hold still." In fact, the story of remarkable heroics was false.

Army Captain Linda Bray commanded a military police company that was ordered to secure a dog kennel belonging to the Panamanian Defense Forces. She competently performed the mission. She and her soldiers came under sporadic fire from snipers hidden in nearby woods, but captured the unoccupied kennel with no American casualties. Enemy body count: seven dogs. Delighted by the novelty of women serving in a combat zone, the press eagerly exaggerated their encounters with the enemy, and the Pentagon and the White House played along. Press secretary Marlin Fitzwater declared the kennel assault "an important military operation" and heralded its female commander.

The Pentagon realized that its attempt to win a little favorable publicity had gotten out of hand when one major newspaper pronounced Captain Bray's actions "worthy of a young Douglas MacArthur or George Patton." The Army's belated attempt to correct the absurd exaggeration was in vain. In an unwitting female Army captain, feminists had the symbol they wanted to advance their cause.

A year later the Gulf War provided the propaganda feminists would again use to intimidate critics. The largest deployment of women in history prompted such media attention that the public could be forgiven for thinking that women were largely responsible for the swift victory, although they made up only 6 percent of the force.

About forty thousand women were deployed to the Gulf, where five died in hostile fire when their barracks was hit by a Scud missile. Seizing on any available casualties, feminists equated these passive victims in a combat zone with the death of soldiers directly engaged in mortal combat with the enemy.

In her feminist brief for equal rights in the military, *Ground Zero: The Gender Wars in the Military*, Linda Bird Francke examined lessons supposedly learned in both Panama and the Gulf War. She relied on random experiences of a handful of women soldiers, the testimony of a platoon of embittered female veterans, and the advocacy of the Pentagon's feminist lobby to build a case for women in combat. She explained that military women are condemned to second-class status by a misogynist military culture, which refuses to recognize women's allegedly proven ability to engage in combat.

Francke ignores uncomfortable facts about the deployment of women to the Gulf that contradict her feminist case for combat integration. A General Accounting Office study of soldiers called up to serve in the Gulf War found that women were four times more nondeployable than men owing to pregnancy and family responsibilities. Sailors are supposed to be celibate at sea. But a woman serving in the military is not merely an extension of her working outside the home. Men and women in the military sleep where they work— often together as we have learned. The USS *Acadia* was dubbed the "Love Boat" by the media when 10 percent of its 360 female sailors had to be evacuated owing to pregnancies during the Gulf War. A Roper poll found that 64 percent of Gulf War veterans who served in mixed-gender units reported there had been sexual activity between men and women in their units. A majority said that the sexual relationships had a negative effect on their units' morale.

Francke asserted that when two female American POWs were safely returned, "Iraqi forces had reassured the American public about the viability of women in combat." But the public barely had time to react when the young female truck driver POW, held five weeks, returned and reported that she had received a marriage proposal from an Iraqi officer. The fact that both women had been sexually molested by their Iraqi captors would not be revealed for another year.

The other female POW was Major Rhonda Cornum, an Army flight surgeon and a proponent of women in combat, who explained in her book about her ordeal that her two broken arms and a bullet in her shoulder had not prevented an Iraqi guard from molesting her on the first of her seven days in captivity. Major Cornum dismissed her experience in a surgeon's clinical terms, explaining, "I was manually molested, anally and vaginally," and remains an outspoken advocate of women in combat.

While feminists took false solace in the public's lack of reaction to unknown facts, they were alarmed at the negative reaction to the deployment of mothers. Until 1975, women were removed from the service for pregnancy or even stepmotherhood. Francke explains that to feminists, "interchangeability of father/mother roles is essential to downplay a mother's indispensability to her young children and thereby allow her to pursue a guilt-free life outside the home." But as the evening news chronicled mothers leaving babies as young as six weeks of age to head to the Gulf, the public rejected the feminists' "interchangeability" theory of parenthood and flooded Capitol Hill with protests.

Numerous bills were introduced ordering the Pentagon to bring home from the Gulf single parents and one member of any dual-career military couple with children and exempt them from combat deployments. The public recognized that all military dependent children risk losing a parent, but no child should face the risk of being orphaned by the loss of a sole parent or both parents. In an AP poll, 64 percent of the public agreed that it was "unacceptable for the United States to send women with young children to the war zone."

CHILDREN THE CASUALTIES

Single custodial parents in the military are disproportionately female, and the public clearly saw a distinction between the sacrifices of mothers and the sacrifices of fathers. Someone must fight our wars, so some fathers will inevitably be at risk; but must young mothers be exposed to the dangers of combat? The relatively short deployment and low casualty rate prevented the bills from becoming law. When then Secretary of Defense Dick Cheney notified Congress of the Pentagon's opposition to a bill that would remove "key personnel" from war zones, he explained, "The only reason we exist is to be prepared to fight and win wars. We're not a social welfare agency." But single custodial parents are welcomed in the military, and so our lean, mean fighting machine runs the largest day care system in the world.

Twelve years later, the public isn't being asked its opinion about the deployment of mothers, and a mother of six is celebrated as the very model of a dedicated modern soldier. And some women in uniform do see the military as a social welfare agency. California National Guard Sergeant Sharon Stallworth, thirty-six, could be in Iraq for eighteen months. As a news account about the single mother pointed out, "The military has provided Sharon Stallworth with a living wage and a promising career path—both hard to find when you have six kids and no college degree." When she first deployed, her five-year-old daughter spent weeks sitting in a chair clutching a picture of her mother. Black women like Stallworth make up 12.7 percent of the female population, but represent 34 percent of the military's female enlisted personnel.

When she signed up for the National Guard ten years ago, Sharon Stallworth didn't expect to ever have to leave her six children in the care of their grandmother for months on end. "We do floods and fires," she told her mother.[11]

In addition to the historic number of female veterans with physical injuries, the military health care system is treating a disproportionate number of women returning from overseas assignments with post-traumatic stress disorder (PTSD). According to *The Chicago Tribune,* "One children's book increasingly popular among military families illustrates what the effects of this most recent war might mean for society in the years and even decades to come: *Why Is Mommy Like She Is? A Book for Kids About PTSD.*"[12]

Male veterans also suffer from PTSD, but in yet another unwelcome difference between the sexes, "female troops appear more prone to post-traumatic stress disorder, or PTSD, than their male counterparts," and "studies indicate that many of these women suffer from more pronounced and debilitating forms of PTSD than men."[13]

Following the Gulf War, studies found that female veterans were twice as likely as male troops to develop PTSD, which reflects the two-to-one ratio of female-to-male PTSD sufferers in the general population. "Researchers [at the VA's Clinical Neurosciences Division in West Haven, Connecticut] have found female brains may be less efficient than male brains at producing the neurosteroids that help human beings cope with stress. Other studies have shown that women deplete serotonin, a substance that helps combat depression, more quickly than men and regenerate it more slowly."[14]

In arguing that the mommy-goes-to-war issue was put to rest by the Gulf War, Francke fails to recognize that her discussion of the issue chronicles widespread child neglect aided and abetted by the military. Members of the active-duty military have 1.6 million children, half of whom are under the age of six. During *peacetime,* military mothers complain about the inadequacy of the services' child-care centers, which are open only twelve hours a day. The Gulf War gave rise to the phenomenon of pediatric postwar syndrome: A significant number of children of deployed parents suffered sleep disorders, discipline problems, and weaker attachments to their parents. Francke approvingly notes that the modern military is increasingly "a particular mecca for single parents." For many vulnerable single mothers, the military provides a tempting safety net of benefits, including health care and housing.

During a quieter time, in early 2001, the *Arkansas Democrat-Gazette* told the story of one such vulnerable single mother. Mayzola "Angel" Seals, age thirty-three, "is an example of the new kind of recruit the Army is seeking." It was reported that Seals was struggling to figure out how to pay off $17,000 in student loans, raise two children alone, and hold a job with reasonable hours. The Army came to her "rescue." It offered to pay off her loans, pay her tuition to finish school, and added an $8,000 bonus. The single mother signed up. Single mothers, like Sharon Stallworth and Angel Seals, are finding the male support feminists insist they don't need in Uncle Sam's ranks.

MY SERVICE IN THE PENTAGON'S GENDER WAR

Congresswoman Pat Schroeder eagerly pounced on the "proof" that women were combat-ready by proposing a four-year test of combat integration following the Panama engagement. When the quick, successful Gulf War looked like the kind of high-tech engagement American troops could count on in the future, and with press accounts exaggerating women's role in the conflict, Representative Schroeder tried to lift the services' combat exemptions for women.

The assault on Baghdad in 2003 and the bloody house-by-house fighting in Fallujah the following year should lay to rest the notion that war-fighting in this high-tech age is substantially different than in the past. It remains violent, bloody, and physically demanding.

Every service chief recognized the physical demands of combat and publicly opposed putting women in combat units, but feminist intimidation prompted Congress to lift the exemption for combat aircraft. Women would be permitted to serve in air combat at the services' discretion. Congress got out of the line of feminist fire and drafted the Pentagon to fight off the feminists. It established the Presidential Commission on the Assignment of Women in the Armed Forces to study "the legal, military and societal implications of amending the exclusionary laws."

I was a member of the presidential commission, which spent 1992 conducting hearings to solicit expert testimony from men and women in the military, scientists, medical specialists, and academics. Elaine Donnelly, a conservative veteran of the Pentagon's gender wars as a Reagan appointee to the Defense Advisory Committee on Women in the Services, also served on the commission. Donnelly is a tireless advocate for a strong military and deeply committed to the best interests of military men and women. Her supporters and sources throughout the ranks in all the services have learned to rely on her discretion and sound judgment. Her meticulous research, formidable debating skills, and disarming charm make her one of the most effective advocates for any cause.

A Michigan native, Donnelly joined the fight against the ERA as a young mother with two little girls. When the feminists were meeting in Houston in 1977 to celebrate International Women's Year at their taxpayer-funded conference, she was across town at the Houston Astro Arena as part of Phyllis Schlafly's "Pro-Life, Pro-Family" counterrally. She recalls being energized by the eleven thousand women and their families who resolved to return home and get involved in grassroots politics. She notes the irony that Bella Abzug hoped to mobilize women and she did—by convincing Elaine Donnelly and thousands like her that they should engage in politics and public policy.

Over the years, Donnelly became increasingly concerned about the effects of social engineering on the military and in 1993 founded the Center for Military Readiness, based in Livonia, Michigan, which wields an influence at the Pentagon and in Congress far beyond its size. She has been sued and scorned in vain attempts to silence her. During the commission's work, I would witness her cool logic and fearlessness in the face of fierce feminist attacks and worry that her courage and fortitude undermined the case against putting women in combat.

The commission reviewed historical and current research on the subject and surveyed retired and active-duty members of the military. In early 1992, each service chief publicly testified that he opposed assigning women to combat. In addition to voicing their concerns about the negative effects on combat readiness and unit cohesion, Air Force Chief of Staff Merrill McPeak flatly declared, "I don't think old men should send young women to war."

For months, the commission wrangled over which principle should guide our deliberations when the demands of equal opportunity conflicted with the imperative for combat effectiveness. Along with the Pentagon's chief tormentor Pat Schroeder and its in-house feminist lobby, the retired female careerists who angrily monitored our careful deliberations clearly believed that the military should bear any burden to advance the careers of women in uniform. The only women in uniform who reliably agreed with them were frustrated female pilots in the Navy who believed their inability to fly combat missions limited their promotion prospects. Women in the Army and Marine Corps, officer and enlisted alike, opposed their involuntary assignment to ground combat in order to advance the careers of the Navy's golden girls who wanted to fly with the guys.

When I asked a young enlisted woman her opinion of women serving in combat during a visit to a Marine base, she replied, "Not if it's not good for the Corps, ma'am." Unlike the careerists who lobbied the commission to lift the exemption, this young Marine had internalized the Corps' ethic of the welfare of the group trumping the desires or ambitions of an individual.

DOUBLE STANDARDS

I quickly learned that the demand for equal opportunity was a typically dishonest feminist ruse. Advocates for women in combat were really seeking special rights for women in uniform. They argued that women should be allowed to serve in combat if they felt like it, although men are involuntarily assigned to combat duties. And feminists weren't demanding an equal right for women to compete to meet the services' physical standards. They were demanding a new separate physical standard for women because the great majority can't meet a male standard.

Definitive studies show that the top 5 percent of women perform at the male medium. The average twenty- to thirty-year-old woman has the aerobic capacity of a fifty-year-old man. There's a reason why fifty-year-old men in uniform are not expected to do what twenty-year-old men do. To mask these real differences between the sexes, with their real consequences in the real world of combat—under pressure to integrate the ranks—the services have modified their training.

Since it was integrated, in a typical example of how the military copes with the fact that women are weaker and slower than men, West Point has developed a formula of "equivalent effort" that has male cadets obliged to complete an obstacle course in 3:20 minutes, while female cadets are allowed 5:30. Men receive the same grade for doing seventy-two push-ups in two minutes as women do for performing forty-eight. Scores on fitness tests throughout the military are now similarly "gender-normed."

The physical qualifications for specific jobs have also had to be changed to accommodate the lesser physical strength of women. A 1985 Navy study found that large majorities of women were unable to perform any of eight critical shipboard tasks that virtually all men could handle. To keep things shipshape on the gender front, the job of stretcher carrier in the Navy, once a two-man job (that 100 percent of men but only 12 percent of women could perform) was redefined as a four-person task.

Proponents of women in combat are tiresome in their dishonest insistence that women should only serve on the front lines "if they can meet all the physical requirements." Experience with integrating the service academies and the great majority of specialties has shown that women can't and don't meet the male standard. The force is slower and weaker as a result.

In 1998, the British military abandoned its "gender-fair" policy of gender-norming scores on physical tests in favor of a "gender-free" policy that set the same standards for men and women. The gender-blind policy led to "record levels of injuries." Prior to the change, female trainees suffered 467 injuries per 10,000; with "gender-free" training, women's injuries went up to 1,113 per 10,000. Seven years later, our British allies reinstituted the policy that takes into account the sexes' different physical abilities.[15]

Recent press accounts have military women determinedly doing what is asked of them despite their physical limitations. When Army Private Teresa Broadwell's MP unit came under fire in Karbala, the twenty-year-old provided covering fire from the turret of her Humvee. At five feet three inches, she was too short to see through the sight of her machine gun, so she gauged the accuracy of her fire by watching the tracer rounds. A male colleague noted, "If she were two inches taller, it would have helped, but you couldn't expect anything more."[16] Her mother told *Reader's Digest* that Teresa had to be bulked up in order to join the military. "She weighed 94 pounds. We had to get her up to 100."[17]

Private first class Melissa Castillo, an eighteen-year-old from Queens, New York, was killed in a training exercise in South Korea in 2003 when the personnel carrier she was driving rolled over. She was improperly seated and wasn't wearing a seat belt. The five-foot, two-inch Castillo had removed her seat back and placed it on her vehicle seat to boost herself high enough to see. An accident report explained that the driver of the vehicle she was in had to be at least five feet five inches to see obstacles on the road ahead.[18]

The double standard demanded by feminists isn't confined to physical tests. In 1997, when Air Force lieutenant Kelly Flinn faced a court-martial on charges of adultery, lying under oath, and disobeying a direct order after she was caught having an affair with the husband of an enlisted woman, feminists rallied to her defense. Flinn was the first female B-52 bomber pilot. When she violated military regulations, she and her feminist supporters immediately cried that she shouldn't be treated like one of the guys. The previous year, sixty men and seven women had been prosecuted by the Air Force for adultery. In addition to the adultery charge, which she denied in a written sworn statement, Flinn disobeyed a direct order from her commander to stay away from her married boyfriend. Congresswoman Nita Lowey of New York complained that "the Air Force should have offered Kelly Flinn counseling, warnings, and a transfer." In short, Flinn should have gotten special treatment.

Flinn, an Air Force Academy graduate certified to fly armed with nuclear weapons, waged an unprecedented public relations campaign against the Air Force and adopted a "what's a poor girl supposed to do" defense. A misty-eyed Flinn told *60 Minutes*, "I was twenty-five years old at the time and . . . very confused." Overnight the Air Force's golden girl was a helpless victim being treated badly because she had fallen in love with the wrong guy.

Misplaced sympathy for Flinn shifted to where it belonged when the wronged wife, a junior enlisted woman who noted that she couldn't compete with the glamorous female pilot, publicly complained about Flinn's refusal to stay away from her husband. Feminism has not yet managed to make the traditional, sympathetic image of a betrayed wife appear archaic or ridiculous. The first female Air Force secretary ultimately gave Flinn a less than honorable discharge rather than a court-martial, and another feminist myth was shattered. Kelly Flinn hadn't made it as a pioneer pilot in a man's world because ultimately she refused to be held to its standards.

The presidential commission built a detailed record supporting the combat exemption for women, which rested on the negative effect integration would have on combat effectiveness. The costs of integrating women into combat far outweighed any measurable benefits beyond the dishonest claim of "equal rights." On November 15, 1992, a well-documented report was sent to the president. By a narrow margin, the commission recommended permitting women to serve on combat ships, except submarines and amphibious vessels where the confined conditions raised serious privacy concerns. A majority recommended that the Pentagon retain the "Risk Rule" that prohibited assigning women to units that would expose them to risk of combat or capture.

By a narrow margin, the commission recommended against integrating combat aircraft, and unanimous votes opposed integrating ground combat and Special Forces. In opposing the integration of combat air, I was persuaded by the kind of testimony the commission heard recounting the experiences of pilots who flew over North Vietnam. "In the short time it took [Vietnam POW Lance

Sijan] to parachute to earth, he would travel from the relative security of the twentieth century's most advanced military technology to a jungle where the rules and conduct of combat had not undergone any major alteration since Neolithic times."[19]

The recommendations were largely ignored. One of the incoming Clinton administration's top priorities was its own assault on military culture with the president's proposal to lift the ban on homosexuals serving in the military. Later, Duke University law professor Madeline Morris would serve as a "consultant on gender integration" to Bill Clinton's Army secretary. She advised him that the military must eliminate its "masculinist attitudes" such as "dominance, assertiveness, aggressiveness, independence, self-sufficiency, and willingness to take risks." What had to be eliminated were the masculine qualities that make for an effective fighting force. Pat Schroeder's shock troops were now in civilian control of the military.

FEMINISTS SINK THE NAVY

But before there was Madeline Morris, there was Barbara Pope, who served as an assistant secretary of the Navy for manpower in President George H. W. Bush's administration. In 1992, Pope joined with other feminist advocates of women in combat who exploited a raucous party of naval aviators in Las Vegas to force a surrender by the Navy's top brass that sent women closer to the front lines. "We are in the process of weeding out the white male as norm," Pope explained. "We are about changing the culture."[20]

Following the Tailhook convention in September 1991, a female admiral's aide, Navy lieutenant Paula Coughlin, alleged that she had been sexually assaulted by drunken officers. The annual conventions of the Tailhook Association, run by active-duty and retired Navy pilots, had gotten more raucous with each passing year. In the evenings, there was too much alcohol, too much testosterone, and too many willing young women anxious to party with handsome aviators, and the get-together became a drunken bacchanal.

Lieutenant Coughlin, who had been lobbying on Capitol Hill in favor of repealing the combat exemption for aviation a few weeks before the convention, said she was assaulted in a hallway by a "gauntlet" of drunken pilots who pawed women as they passed by. During the ensuing investigation she was unable to identify her attackers, but by the time her case fell apart, a major case against the Navy and its culture was being prosecuted.

By April 1992 the Navy had conducted 2,200 interviews and produced a two-thousand-page report. When only forty-four incidents that provided enough evidence to warrant disciplinary action were identified, Pat Schroeder alleged a cover-up and indicted the Navy as a whole. She declared that the sexual harassment of women at the convention was caused by a Navy culture that failed to treat women as fully equal. Barbara Pope agreed. They both illogically argued that the remedy for the mistreatment of women at that Las Vegas hotel was lifting the combat exemption and exposing women to violence at the hands of enemy troops.

When yet another report was issued a year later, again I found myself on CNN's *Crossfire*, this time debating Barbara Pope about the appropriate response to the despicable but isolated behavior at the Tailhook convention. Pope saw the patriarchy at fault. I explained that I didn't think the remedy to being mistreated by drunken aviators was to expose American women to far worse treatment at the hands of enemy soldiers. "There's two different issues because a two-track system that treats women as second-class citizens and allows some men to think they're second-class is never going to improve," Pope retorted.

A few months later, I met a grateful naval officer at a Washington conference who noted that I was willing to defend the Navy when its senior officers weren't and predicted that I "would never have to pay for a drink at an officers' club." He made reference to a point I made in this debate with Barbara Pope, who was one of the top civilians then running the Navy. "[The Navy leadership] have allowed the entire Navy to be indicted and pled guilty to sexual harassment. . . . They have somehow made everybody in the Navy guilty until proven innocent, and I think that is a shame. People in the Navy deserve better than that from their senior leadership. They are now in this orgy of atonement. They're battle-fatigued in the gender wars, and they're running up the white flag. The only way they can make it up to Pat Schroeder and the feminists, and I'm afraid Barbara Pope, is by putting women in combat. They are selling out the men in uniform."[21]

Despite an exhaustive investigation and the Navy's desperate desire to appease feminists, there was simply not enough evidence of actual assaults to warrant criminal prosecutions. But plenty of male officers were punished anyway. The careers of fourteen admirals and nearly three hundred naval aviators were ended or damaged by Tailhook. The Senate demanded that the Navy identify any officer connected to the infamous convention by maintaining a Tailhook "blacklist" of seventy-three officers. The list included forty-five men who had either been cleared or never charged with wrongdoing. Many of the others had received a minor rebuke not intended to be part of an officer's permanent record. Presence on the "blacklist" prevented promotion.

Commander Bob Stumpf never achieved the fame of media darling Paula Coughlin, but he was the real victim of Tailhook. Stumpf was awarded the Distinguished Flying Cross for his heroic performance during the Gulf War. The former commander of the Navy's Blue Angels elite flight team was at the convention to accept a "best in the Navy" award on behalf of his squadron. An administrative hearing unanimously cleared him of any wrongdoing. He didn't take part in any of the debauchery, and no one even identified him as a witness to any of the outrageous behavior. When his promotion was repeatedly blocked, he left the Navy. Sexual politics denied the Navy the service of one of its finest officers, and an ungrateful nation he had put his life on the line to defend permitted this war hero to be shamefully mistreated.

By the summer of 1992, after months of taking incoming fire over the Tailhook scandal, the Navy surrendered and dropped its opposition to repealing the exemption for combat ships. Men with chests full of medals attesting to their physical bravery were no match for shrill feminists demanding tribute.

Feminists don't care a whit about Commander Bob Stumpf's heroic service because he belongs to the guilty class of white males and exhibits despised masculine traits. The feminist project to integrate all forms of combat denies the history of warfare that shows masculine traits are vital to military success. Historian S.L.A. Marshall found that a man in combat will overcome his fear and do what's required because he risks losing "the one thing that he is likely to value more highly than life—his reputation as a man among other men."

But when Bill Clinton's top personnel official for the Army trashed the Marine Corps, it quickly became clear that she had picked on the wrong guys. In Baltimore in 1997, at an academic conference on the relationship between the military and civilian society, Sara Lister, assistant secretary of the army for manpower and reserve affairs, said, "The Marines are extremists. Wherever you have extremists, you've got some risks of total disconnection with society, and that's a little dangerous. . . . The Marine Corps is—you know, they have all these checkerboard fancy uniforms and stuff. But the Army is sort of muddy boots on the ground." Appearing on the same panel as Assistant Secretary Lister, I objected to her depiction of the Marines and was particularly rankled that she was offering her disgraceful assessment as a representative of the Army my husband had served in for over twenty years.

After the seminar, I got a copy of the taped proceedings and shared it with people who I thought would be interested in this senior Army official's opinion of the Marines. Lister was an enthusiastic proponent of opening combat positions to women, and her candid remarks obviously reflected her own extremist view of those who most strenuously resisted her agenda. The commandant of the Marine Corps vehemently objected to her comments, saying they dismissed "222 years of sacrifice and dedication." Her apology, claiming her statements were "taken out of context," satisfied Secretary of Defense Bill Cohen ("This issue is over") but failed to quell the controversy. The House unanimously passed a resolution calling on Lister to resign—and she did. It was a rare victory for defenders of the military's warrior culture during Bill (and Hillary's) years, when feminists and the men who fear them were in charge of the Pentagon.

NEW YORK'S BRAVEST DEFEND STANDARDS

There is a telling recent example of dangerous men's work being done free of coercive social engineering. The heroes of 9/11 provided a rare opportunity to celebrate the masculine traits that drove those firemen—not firefighters—into the burning towers to do the dangerous, demanding, dirty work of men. "These are the men who will fight our wars," President Bush proclaimed when he visited the smoldering recovery scene in lower Manhattan.

There are only 26 women among the 11,500-member force of New York's Bravest. A federal judge found in 1982 that the fire department's physical test for applicants improperly discriminated against women and ordered the department to water down its requirements. Determined to maintain standards that met its mission's requirements, the New York City Fire Department instituted a modified test that remains demanding enough that more than 40 percent of male applicants fail to make the grade. There are no gender-normed scores and no gender quotas on hiring.

Commenting on the pressure to be more diverse by welcoming women in their ranks, an official at New York State's Fire Academy candidly explains, "They're accepted because they have to be accepted, not because they are considered to be equal in their abilities. The men have to say, 'Yes, there are women who can do the job and I wouldn't mind trusting my safety to a female the same way I would to a male.'"[22]

In 2000, New York City's fire department stopped issuing individual safety ropes as part of a fireman's basic equipment owing to complaints about the added weight. The department reconsidered its decision following two deaths and serious injuries among six firemen who were trapped on the roof of a Bronx building in January 2005.[23]

A fireman's basic gear weighs fifty-nine pounds, the "can man" carries a total of ninety-six pounds, and a "roof firefighter" is weighted down with 130 pounds. The land combat soldier carries weapons and equipment weighing fifty to one hundred pounds, with body armor alone weighing twenty-five pounds. For the military, in the lull of peacetime, equal opportunity trumped combat effectiveness. There is never a peacetime for the firemen of New York.

With the risks firemen face so obvious, and the prospect that even a feminist on Manhattan's Upper West Side might have to count on their reckless bravery, there were no feminist protests when there wasn't a pleasing gender balance among the 343 brave firemen who died on 9/11.

7 | The Gender Gap Debunked

In light of the damage wrought over the past thirty years, the most costly investment Congress ever made handed $5 million to feminists in 1976 to fund state meetings and then a three-day national convention. It was "International Women's Year," which called for a political agenda to tackle sexual inequality. This first-ever women's convention in 1977 produced the left-wing agenda that feminists have been pushing ever since.

In a preview of that feminist fest in Houston, former congresswoman Bella Abzug (D–NY), who would preside over the affair, and actress Jean Stapleton, who was "television's classic housewife"[1] because of her role as Edith Bunker in the TV series *All in the Family*, made it clear that they would not be engaging in a charm offensive to advance their political demands. The tools of choice to hammer politicians would be wielded by feminist political activists and their female friends in the media. They would use disinformation, intimidation, and the feminists' favorite political fable—the supposed gender gap in voting that threatened any candidate who didn't knuckle under to their agenda.

Women opposed to feminist orthodoxy had been badly outnumbered at many of the state sessions held around the country in 1977. Although the entire endeavor culminating in Houston was billed by feminists as a "Constitutional Convention for Women,"[2] the process wasn't going to be an intellectually stimulating example of democracy in action. A rigid orthodoxy would be enforced. Abzug expressed the feminists' slanderous dismissal of anyone who didn't conform to their monolithic views. "In some states there were disruption attempts by the ultra-right, like the Ku Klux Klan, who still want to keep their women home washing the sheets," she angrily declared.[3] Stapleton announced that Edith Bunker would support the stalled Equal Rights Amendment, "if she understood it." This contempt and condescension and the claim that only sexists and simpletons oppose their "women's agenda" are characteristic of feminist politics.

THE BATTLE OVER THE ERA

Ratification of the Equal Rights Amendment (ERA) was the top priority of the two thousand delegates and an estimated eleven thousand onlookers at the federally funded convention in Houston in November 1977. The ERA had sailed through Congress in 1972, with lawmakers assured that it enjoyed the virtually unanimous support of American women. The House approved it by a margin of 354 to 23 and the Senate by 84 to 8. Over the following year, it was enthusiastically ratified by thirty states, only eight states shy of the three quarters needed to amend the Constitution during the seven-year time limit. But conservative stalwart Phyllis Schlafly and her own army of women, the National Committee to Stop ERA, were just getting started.

Long before the modern women's movement got under way, Phyllis Schlafly was making her own way. She earned a graduate degree in political science from Radcliffe in 1945. Back home in St. Louis she worked for a local bank writing speeches for its executives and making a few of her own on investment and estate planning to women audiences. An early press notice described the "blonde banking expert" as a "forceful speaker."[4] In 1952, now living in Illinois, she ran unsuccessfully for Congress as an "average housewife" and a strong anti-Communist in favor of increased defense spending. She and Eisenhower both lost in the predominantly Democratic district.

Schlafly remained active in politics and interested in national issues, particularly national security, as she raised a family of six children. Her 1964 book *A Choice Not an Echo* took on the liberal wing of the Republican party, rallied support to Barry Goldwater, and was the bestselling political book of that election year. Her three books on national security published during the 1960s sold over 2.5 million copies. She testified before Congress as a critic of arms control treaties and was prepared to talk about defense policy before a conservative group in Connecticut in 1971 but was told the group wanted to hear about the pending ERA. Schlafly read up on the proposed amendment and decided she opposed it. The STOP ERA movement was born.

The ERA was sold by feminists as a remedy for women's "second-class citizenship," but Schlafly persuasively argued that women enjoyed every constitutional right that men enjoyed and challenged its supporters to identify any specific discrimination against women that the amendment would eliminate. She portrayed it as a dangerous transfer of power over laws traditionally within the province of states to federal judges and a distant Washington, and explained that it threatened to eliminate protections women enjoyed. When I debated the issue in the late seventies with feminists like Karen De-Crow, the president of NOW (1974–1977), as a newly minted lawyer, I found that even their veteran attorneys were unable to defend the ERA's misleadingly simple language because its potential for mischief was clear and its full effects were unknowable.

By the time the delegates gathered in Houston, approval of the ERA had stalled. It had been endorsed by President Gerald Ford, whose wife, along with Lady Bird Johnson and Rosalynn Carter, joined the sisterhood on the conference stage. Mrs. Carter adopted the requisite dismissive tone toward anyone who parted ways with the program. "We should say to those who are wavering because they are ill-informed or confused or because of shrill voices: 'You should think about yourself.'"[5] President Jimmy Carter had appointed Bella Abzug to preside over the public conferences in honor of International Women's Year. Her appointment looked like a consolation prize. A veteran antiwar activist, Abzug had been elected to Congress in 1970, but lost Senate and mayoral primaries in 1976 and 1977.

Feminists had their flamboyant leader and their federal funds. They claimed to have 450 groups, representing 50 million Americans, pining for the ERA. That year, Indiana would become the thirty-fifth (and last) state to ratify the ERA.

Frustrated that they had been unable to make their sale despite their friends in high places, Hollywood supporters, and significant resources, feminists insisted on changing the ratification rules. The following year, Congress extended the deadline for ratification for another three years by a significantly less enthusiastic vote than the ERA had enjoyed six years earlier. After ten years, the ERA finally died on June 30, 1982. A total of five states that had ratified it rescinded their ratification. It was not a predictable fate for an amendment allegedly favored by over half the population. The experience should have taught lawmakers that feminists wrongly claim to speak for American women, but lawmakers have been slow learners. Bella Abzug expressed her own contempt for the allegedly powerful patriarchy when she said, "The establishment is made up of little men, very frightened."

The twenty-five-point plan of action adopted in Houston also included government-funded abortion on demand, a massive federal day care program, a comparable-worth scheme, lesbian rights, the elimination of nuclear weapons arsenals, and a Cabinet-level Women's Department. In celebratory dispatches, women reporters declared their solidarity with the delegates. Sally Quinn wrote about the novelty of the all-female get-together, "Their voices were merry and high-pitched. In fact the whole lobby sounded like the middle of a bird cage, with all the chirping sounds of women's voices."[6] Ignoring any specifics about the plan of action, and evidently surprised that not every woman in attendance looked like Bella Abzug, Quinn observed admiringly, "Somewhere between the feminist meetings of five years ago and now, the radical feminists had lost control, and Middle America had gotten its grip on things."

When she ventured across town to check out Phyllis Schlafly's pro-family counterconvention of eleven thousand meeting at the Astro Arena, Quinn didn't see Middle America. She saw besotted Schlafly-worshipers who "came in their chartered buses and church vans from all over East Texas and Tennessee . . . with their bibles, their flags and their signs." She saw bigots who were there "to show their disgust for the lesbians, perverts and baby killers meeting across town."[7] Schlafly, with her "blonde spit curls," knew the "trigger words" that would "whip them up into a fervor."[8] It was clear that Quinn thought certain women should just stay at home.

And Bella? In a classic example of the favorable portraits feminists can typically count on, the loud, obnoxious politician was nowhere in evidence in Houston, according to Quinn. "She was softer, warmer, easier, more mellow, funnier than ever before."[9]

THE PHONY GENDER GAP IS BORN

In 1980, Middle America elected Ronald Reagan, who opposed the ERA. More women voted for the conservative former governor than for the incumbent president who had been one of the feminists' most ardent suitors. Reagan beat Carter by twenty points among men (56 to 36 percent) and edged him out among women 47 to 45 percent. The difference in the level of support between men and women created a nine-point gender gap. The notion that this difference would be a permanent disadvantage for Republicans was aggressively promoted.

One Democratic strategist announced "there were now two political parties in the United States: One was the women's party, and the other wished it were the women's party."[10] Feminists claimed that offending their sensibilities spelled political doom at the polls. Only politicians who endorsed abortion rights at home and pacifism abroad could avoid defeat at the hands of angry women voting their victimhood.

Ann Lewis, as political director of the Democratic National Committee, exclaimed, "The gender gap is the Grand Canyon of American politics. It is wide, it is deep and it is beautiful." Lewis predicted that women voters would support Democrats by a margin of twelve points in 1984.[11]

Women journalists joined the sisterhood's chorus. Helen Thomas, the UPI's White House reporter, specialized in the siren call for Democrats to listen to the ladies because President Reagan's deaf ear was causing him big trouble. "Reagan's polls in recent months," she wrote in 1983, "show that he is not as popular with women as he is with men." Citing no evidence at all, she went on, "His opposition to the Equal Rights Amendment has hurt him with working women."[12] Later in the year, Thomas claimed "Reagan is running into obstacles in his quest for the women's vote." Thomas noted that Reagan's "firsts," the appointment of Sandra Day O'Connor to the Supreme Court and Jeane Kirkpatrick as ambassador to the UN, didn't do the trick. Again, the bald assertion: "But the White House is learning that the problem is much broader, and that Reagan's opposition to the Equal Rights Amendment hurt his image with the modern day American woman who believes there is still discrimination in many areas." And a warning: "With the elections more than a year away, Reagan still has a chance to make many affirmative moves to improve his image with women, but it may require a philosophical change of direction."[13]

Columnist Ellen Goodman shared the feminists' assumption that women could be expected to support a woman candidate. "The figures emerging out of the gender gap look pretty good for a female candidate," she explained, because more women than men would be voting. Goodman echoed the feminists' conviction that it was about time to put a woman on the Democratic ticket to take advantage of all that female hostility to the incumbent president.[14]

In early 1984, Bella Abzug asserted "that women do join across all racial, social, and regional lines in stark opposition to President Reagan and his policies." She confidently predicted that the women's vote would defeat the president in the fall. Eleanor Smeal, the former president of NOW, wrote a book titled *Why and How Women Will Elect the Next President* crediting the feminist movement for Reagan's alleged women trouble. The gender gap as defined by the feminists fueled their argument that putting a woman on the ticket in 1984 was just the ticket for electoral success.

MONDALE PICKS A WOMAN AND LOSES WOMEN

The Smeal ideological analysis on how to defeat President Reagan sounded like a holy war and was wholly wrong. She insisted that the women's vote would make the decisive difference and cited a study she conducted for the Democrats that found choosing a female running mate would boost the savvy candidate by 10 points in the polls. She predicted that the issue of abortion would be paramount that year because "once the public understands that Mr. Reagan's anti-abortion position is against all abortion they will rally to the other side." Again, this strident ideologue was in friendly hands, with a woman reporter pointing out that "NOW no longer carries the radical label it once flaunted. Ms. Smeal herself may be a large reason for that middle-road respectability. As a mother of two . . . and former full-time homemaker, Ms. Smeal gave the women's movement the appearance of fighting for the average American woman."[15]

Although there was a conspicuous absence of potential female candidates with records that would merit joining a presidential ticket, it was clear that no excuses would be accepted. Judy Goldsmith, the president of NOW, said, "I don't think there is any reason to suggest that there are not a number of women with the records, experience and stature to assume the No. 2 position, and if the politicians don't know that, the public does."[16]

A week before the Democratic convention in San Francisco, NOW passed a resolution stating that its members intended to wage a floor fight if Walter Mondale failed to select a female running mate. A delegation of women visited Mondale at his home in Minnesota to press their case for a woman on the ticket. All of that working on the railroad to force the nomination of a female running mate paid off.

When three-term New York congresswoman Geraldine Ferraro was tapped for the ticket, feminists were jubilant and assumed all women shared their joy. Myra MacPherson of *The Washington Post* saw it as a unifying sisterhood moment, although she quoted Gloria Steinem pointing out that gender solidarity only goes so far. "If it was a Phyllis Schlafly, no one would be celebrating," the feminist icon explained. "It doesn't help to have them look like us—and act like them." MacPherson made it clear she wholeheartedly agreed. "For the first time in America they saw a woman accept the nomination for the vice presidency of the United States. They saw 'one of us.'"[17]

In her column "A Case of Goose Bumps," Ellen Goodman hailed the smart move by Mondale. "We hit one of those rare moments when the right thing to do was also the politically savvy thing to do."[18] "Mr. Mondale mentions the ERA and pay equity in almost every speech," the campaign director for women's issues bragged. Geraldine Ferraro said, "There is a contrast like no other contrast in the history of this country between these two tickets on the issues of concern to women," mentioning war and peace and the environment. The Democrats emphasized their strong support for abortion, comparable worth, the Equal Rights Amendment, and the nuclear freeze.[19] The Republican party was pro-life, opposed to comparable worth, and committed to a strong military.

In his reelection race that November, Ronald Reagan carried 49 states. While Geraldine Ferraro was busy making history on the other ticket, President Reagan was winning over women voters. He beat the Mondale–Ferraro team by a margin of 56 to 44 percent among women and won 62 percent of male voters. The gender gap of 6 points certainly didn't threaten Reagan's landslide. Ann Lewis couldn't have thought it was beautiful.

Following the Reagan rout, feminists showed they weren't the kind of gals who danced with the guy who brought them. Ellen Goodman had been one of many arguing that the "Ferraro factor" could be magic. "But women didn't stop the flow of blood out of the Democratic party from becoming a geyser. Geraldine Ferraro didn't do the impossible: she didn't make Fritz Mondale president," the formerly optimistic Goodman explained, before faulting the Mondale camp because they "played to the women's vote only at the very end."[20]

FEMINISTS CAN'T DO POLITICAL MATH

For over twenty years, the postelection season has been marked by the spectacle of feminists explaining away the failure of their version of the gender gap to sink the Republican candidate. They inevitably insist that the Democratic candidate would have been a sure winner had he talked endlessly about "women's issues." And Republican wins are invariably illegitimate. Congresswoman Pat Schroeder explains that her Congressional Caucus on Women's Issues was going swimmingly "until Newt Gingrich rose to power, riding on the Right-wing seizure of the Republican Party and the House in 1994."[21] Feminists' political theory holds that their issues never lose on the merits and their candidates are never beaten fair and square.

A year after her signature political insight about disgusted women voters rising up against Reagan and voting for a woman in overwhelming numbers was decisively proved wrong, Eleanor Smeal was angrier than ever. "It is time to raise hell against an opposition that is frequently nothing but fascists!" the allegedly mainstream mom announced to a group of union leaders. "I don't enjoy calling people names," Smeal told a reporter, "but from now on we've got to show them for the bigots they are. We've gotta wrap it around their necks!" She bragged, "We are the people who brought you the gender gap."[22]

Republicans have been made to believe that they face intractable women problems, but GOP candidates have been able to bridge a gender divide that remains a treacherous gulf for the Democrats. The Democratic party has been hurt as a result of its feminization at the clenched fists of the feminists in its base.

Analysts at the Democratic Leadership Council have sounded an alarm to their party about the flip side of the GOP's relatively manageable gender gap. Former Clinton White House aide William Galston highlights his party's "White Male Problem." While women have been fickle voters, backing Reagan twice and George H. W. Bush in 1988, but not in 1992, Galston points out that political and policy developments of the past generation have consistently pushed white men away from the Democratic party.

Al Gore received only 36 percent of the white male vote in 2000, John Kerry only 37 percent in 2004. No Democratic presidential candidate has won more than 43 percent of the white male vote since 1976. GOP congressional and gubernatorial candidates also typically win the white male vote by 20-point margins. Democrats' problem with men is far bigger than Republicans' women trouble. Galston explains that "the gender gap is more a reflection of men leaving the Democratic party than of women joining it." Democrats had a 58-point advantage among southern white men in 1952. By 1992, Republicans' 1-point advantage among these men meant there had been a 59-point shift away from the Democrats.

Galston faults the "high-profile extremists" on the left for exacerbating the Democratic party's problems by tagging white men as "racist and patriarchal oppressors." The feminists' rhetoric has been costly. "Republican strength among white men more than offsets Democrats' dominance of the African-American vote," according to Galston. And the party's harridans aren't helping to win over female voters: In a 2001 Gallup poll, only 25 percent of women labeled themselves "feminist." Another survey, by pollster Kellyanne Conway, found 41 percent of women calling themselves "conservative," and only 21 percent "liberal."

Women aren't monolithic voters who fit the feminists' stereotype. A pre-9/11 poll by *The New York Times* on issues most important to the public found women more concerned with missile defense and foreign policy than abortion and gun control. When John Kerry's sister Peggy campaigned for him in Ohio she made a special plea for women voters by detailing his platform on affirmative action, pay equity, child care, and stem cell research. Hollywood feminists, like Sharon Stone and Christine Lahti, chose to insult women's intelligence by taking to the Kerry campaign trail with scary scenarios sure to be realized if George Bush was reelected. Appearing with Oprah, a distraught Cameron Diaz announced, "We have a voice now, and we're not using it, and women have so much to lose. I mean, we could lose the right to our bodies. . . . If you think that rape should be legal, then don't vote."[23]

John Kerry carried the overall women's vote by 3 points, but lost white women voters by 11 points. Kerry lost married women without college degrees by 16 points. These weren't just the much-talked-about "security moms" of post-9/11 America. Since 1980, Democratic presidential candidates have won an average of 46 percent of the white women, two-party vote while Republicans have won an average of 54 percent in those seven national races.

Congresswoman Loretta Sanchez (D–CA) is one of the feminist sirens calling on politicians to ignore the electoral record and heed their take on what women want. "We care about issues that deal with our children and the future of our children. . . . We can identify the women's vote. It is an easy thing to do and about the only way you can get to that woman's vote is to go out there and talk about that record you have on women's issues."[24] George Bush carried married voters with children by nineteen points. "The gap between how white unmarried women vote compared with white married women is a gigantic gap," according to Democratic pollster Stan Greenberg.[25] The marriage gap has been larger than the gender gap in all elections since pollsters have started tracking it.

Women voters as a liberal monolithic group has been the feminists' spin since Eleanor Smeal identified the gender gap twenty-five years ago. Columnist Marianne Means reliably reflects the feminists' agitprop about how to remedy the only version of the gender gap she chooses to recognize. Her typical take: "The gender gap is not so easily overcome. The roots of the trouble lie in Republican policies that women see as threatening. Symbolic gestures and tokenism are inadequate remedies."[26] She is an enthusiastic fan of former governor Christine Todd Whitman's formula for GOP success. "Unless we signal that you can be pro-choice and be a good Republican, we're going to lose a lot of votes," Whitman endlessly warns her party.[27] In her two gubernatorial campaigns in New Jersey, Whitman failed to carry the majority of women voters.

Even when George Bush was soaring in the polls in the spring of 2002, with 76 percent of women giving him positive reviews, Marianne Means was warning him about trouble ahead owing to his pro-life positions.[28] In 2004, Marianne Means was at it again. After tracing the GOP's alleged handicap in appealing to women voters to Ronald Reagan's opposition to the ERA almost twenty-five years earlier, in a column entitled "GOP Since Reagan Just Doesn't Get It," she wrote, "The current campaign repeats past periodic GOP initiatives to persuade female voters that the party's well-hyped male macho attitude does not exclude women—without making any substantive policy changes. And it is destined to be no more successful than they were."[29]

It is Marianne Means who just doesn't get it. In the last seven presidential elections, Republicans have won five times and received more women's votes than Democrats in three of the races.[30]

After offering their bum advice throughout the campaign season, following the 2004 defeat of their candidate, feminists' analysis claimed that John Kerry's failure to discuss "women's issues," including pay equity, paid family leave, and the glass ceiling, cost their guy the race. The quadrennial excuse-makers were out in force. Naomi Wolf gamely shared serial excuses with Katie Couric:

"Event after event John Kerry would appear with nothing but older, white men behind him. . . . He didn't use the moms around him to showcase a message. . . . The Democratic brand is pathetic at using language and imagery," and on and on.[31] Gloria Feldt, former president of Planned Parenthood, faulted the candidate it endorsed for ineffectively defending its radical abortion-rights agenda. "He seemed equivocal. He ceded the moral high ground to the other side," Feldt complained.[32] Even Donna Brazile, Al Gore's campaign manager in 2000, recognized that voters were plenty sure about where John Kerry stood on the issue of abortion. After the 2004 race, she said, "Even I have trouble explaining to my family that we are not about killing babies."[33]

WOMEN VOTERS REJECT "WOMEN'S ISSUES"

Karlyn Bowman, the American Enterprise Institute's polling expert, notes the absence of any polling evidence to indicate that the feminists' agenda was uppermost in women's minds and credits both candidates with talking about the big issues that concerned both men and women. When the Gallup organization asked monthly during 2004 what issues voters cared most about, not even 1 percent mentioned issues like pay equity, child care, or discrimination and violence against women.

In 2003, Gallup looked at the differences between men and women on the big issues. The twenty-eight issues included race relations, environmental quality, poverty, military strength, and the quality of health care. The sexes reported about equal levels of satisfaction and dissatisfaction on most of the issues. There was a difference between the sexes of more than 10 percentage points on only one of the issues. Forty-five percent of men, but only a third of women, were satisfied with the nation's "moral and ethical climate."

On election day, moral values topped the agenda of voters, cited by 43 percent of men and 57 percent of women.[34]

Again, factually challenged feminists ignore the evidence and election results. They stubbornly insist they know what's best for all the women they claim to represent. Looking ahead to George Bush's second term, Marcia Greenberger, co-president of the National Women's Center, said, "What I . . . see is an administration with policies that are fundamentally out of touch with what women really need." In the face of a reelected President Bush and increased GOP majorities, Kim Gandy, president of NOW, wailed, "Our health, our rights, and our democracy are teetering on the brink." Congresswoman Deborah Pryce (R–OH), the highest ranking Republican woman in the House, had a suggestion for Kim Gandy. Pryce thought "an acronym change for the nation's most extreme women's rights group might be in order. 'NOW' is hardly apropos for a group of extremist women who tell other women leading the way in politics, business and education that they're living in male-dominated times. Better we call them 'THEN'—it's obviously where they are stuck."

WOMEN WILD ABOUT BILL

Despite their rejection by women at the polls, feminists stubbornly insist they speak for all women and are wholly committed to representing women's interests. Examples of men behaving badly illustrate how unprincipled feminists are when consistency threatens their ideology and quest for power.

Many of the female candidates who ran for the Senate during the "year of the woman" in 1992 vowed to vindicate the treatment of Anita Hill at the hands of male senators during the Clarence Thomas hearings. Feminists published *The Getting It Gazette* at the

Democratic convention in New York to put men on notice that they were on sexual harassment patrol. They changed their tune by the time elections came around in 1998, the year of the intern.

Like battered women, President Bill Clinton's female supporters were willing to bear any humiliation rather than abandon their guy over Monica Lewinsky. Hillary Clinton rallied the sisterhood to help provide cover for her lying Lothario, and they meekly complied. Former NOW president Patricia Ireland found the preying on a young employee at the office "frustrating" because the scandal was "such a distraction from the key issues that are facing us, questions of public policy and foreign policy." In the midst of the scandal, abortion-rights activist Kate Michelman praised President Clinton for having "the courage of his convictions" on abortion. Republican miscreants have not been treated so gently, because feminist politics trumps feminist principles.

When John Tower was nominated to be secretary of Defense in 1989 and allegations of adultery surfaced, Senator Barbara Mikulski (D–MD) manned the barricades to prevent someone who "so clearly demonstrates disrespect for women" from taking the top Pentagon job. The senator declared, "The phrase 'conduct unbecoming an officer' is an important concept in the U.S. military. It has been applied over the past two hundred years in order to maintain a standard of behavior that inspires respect not only of the military but of its civilians, too. I believe the Senate should apply the same standard to the man who would be second in command in the United States."

Senator Mikulski never explained what the standard should be for the commander-in-chief when she rallied to defend Bill Clinton during his trial in the Senate in 1998. But as a member of the Senate Ethics Committee, she concluded that Senator Bob Packwood should be expelled owing to his "systematic abuse of women, power, and this Senate."

Although Senator Packwood's mistreatment of women became publicly known during his reelection campaign in 1992, it had been well known to his feminist supporters for over twenty years. He grabbed an abortion-rights lobbyist in his office in 1982. She later explained that she did nothing about the assault, and let him continue assaulting other women, because Packwood enthusiastically supported her agenda.

So long as the serial sexual predator was the feminists' faithful friend, his secret was theirs too. Once Packwood was outed, his female colleagues demanded public hearings, and he was forced to resign in 1995. Senator Barbara Boxer saw the recommendation that Packwood be expelled as "a very clear message that the Senate has zero tolerance for the type of behavior he exhibited over the course of his public service." Senator Dianne Feinstein stated that if he was guilty as charged, "his credibility as a United States senator is destroyed. . . . He should resign." It was feminist senators' credibility that was destroyed when they defended Bill Clinton three years later.

Patricia Ireland saw a major message in the Packwood episode. "This has to be a heads-up for men in power. You can't treat women as the spoils of power." Unless you're the husband of a feminist icon, and she's willing to protect you.

Hillary Clinton and her feminist friends served as enablers in exchange for a share in a man's political power—he could abuse his as long as they got to wield theirs. Hillary got to screw around with health care, he got to screw around. When he got caught, she helped to clean up his mess. Such is the pathetic role model feminists urge young women to emulate.

As long as Bill Clinton supported abortion rights, affirmative action, and federal child care, it didn't matter that he was a sexual predator. This wasn't a onetime pass for Bill Clinton alone. More recently, when allegations from his divorce surfaced accusing a Democratic primary candidate in Illinois of physically abusing his former wife, a local feminist was ready to excuse him. Illinois NOW president Bonnie Grabenhofer allowed that the "six-year-old allegations are troubling, but there are still reasons to support [him]." She explained, "Voters need to balance those private allegations with [his] public commitment to women's issues." Grabenhofer cited the candidate's support for abortion rights and Title IX.[35]

There is no monolithic women's vote and there is no monolithic women's agenda. There haven't been since feminists lost their most cherished aim twenty-five years ago. The ERA was defeated when a truth squad, composed largely of women led by Phyllis Schlafly, exposed the threat it posed. Bella Abzug, Eleanor Smeal, Patricia Ireland, and other feminist activists have waged a disinformation campaign to intimidate politicians to support their tired agenda. And like political pamphleteers of old, Helen Thomas, Marianne Means, Ellen Goodman, and other women journalists ignore election results and churn out feminist agitprop to advance the feminist cause. In fact, Republicans can successfully woo women voters, while a feminized Democratic party has lost its male appeal.

8 | Abortion—
the Holy Grail

Modern feminism's biggest enemies are the smallest humans. These activists have made abortion on demand the fundamental right that women's equality depends on. They argue that women can't be the equal of men unless they are free to rid themselves of their unborn children at any time for any reason. Since abortion on demand was elevated to a constitutional right in 1973, these feminists fiercely fight to keep the issue in the courts insulated from public opinion, because the majority of Americans oppose the majority of abortions. Lacking the public's support for their radical abortion agenda, feminists wrap their demands in a tissue of euphemisms and lies and demonize their opponents as misogynist religious zealots.

Feminist fundamentalism holds that the battle of the sexes can't be won unless women make war on the tiniest enemies of their independence. How can women be the equal of men when their bodies betray them? Here abortion advocates reveal their belief that women's fertility makes us inherently inferior to men.

For eighteen years, Kate Michelman headed the premier abortion rights organization that dared not speak its name (NARAL, the innocuous moniker for the National Abortion and Reproductive Rights Action League—now dubbed NARAL Pro-Choice America). She declares, "If women are unable to decide whether and when to have children, they cannot be equal partners in American society, nor can they enjoy the pursuit of happiness that is their sacred right."[1]

Former president of Planned Parenthood Federation of America Gloria Feldt says, "Not only did [Roe v. Wade] legalize abortion but it became a symbol of our independence, because reproductive freedom is fundamental to a woman's aspirations—to education, financial stability, and self-determination. . . . The simple ability to separate sex from childbearing gives women the power to control all other aspects of their lives."[2] Presently, about half of women having abortions are having their second. How's that for control?

Ms. magazine founder Gloria Steinem neatly represents the standard distortion of history, the militant demand for abortion rights, and the ideological dismissal of critics when she writes, "Obviously, reproductive freedom [italics in original] is simply a way of stating what feminism has been advancing for thousands of years. Witches and gypsies were freedom fighters for women because they taught contraception and abortion. It was mainly this knowledge that made them anathema to patriarchs of the past." Feminism's golden girl declares, "But the modern contribution is to elevate reproductive freedom [italics in original] to a universal human right, at least [italics mine] as basic as freedom of speech or assembly." And Steinem sees only villainous opponents to abortion. "Obviously, this reproductive veto power on the part of women is exactly what male supremacists fear most."[3]

PRO-LIFE EARLY FEMINISTS

Today's feminists attempt to ennoble their demands by wrapping themselves in the suffragettes' principled campaign for the right to vote. They argue that you can't be pro-women without being pro-choice. But the radical abortion views of today's feminists like Kate Michelman, Faye Wattleton, Gloria Steinem, Gloria Feldt, and Eleanor Smeal betray the staunchly pro-life views of America's earliest feminists. In fact, those pioneering activists were uniformly opposed to abortion.

Alice Paul founded the National Women's Party in 1915 and authored the Equal Rights Amendment. Her fight for the franchise was depicted in the HBO movie *Iron Jawed Angels*, with Hilary Swank portraying her defiance after being arrested at a protest outside the White House in 1917. Paul believed, "Abortion is the ultimate exploitation of women."[4] There was no disagreement among her fellow suffragettes.

The Revolution, a women's paper published by Susan B. Anthony and Elizabeth Cady Stanton, referred to abortion as "child murder" and "infanticide." In 1869, the weekly declared, "No matter what the motive, love of ease, or a desire to save from suffering the unborn innocent, the woman is awfully guilty who commits the deed. It will burden her conscience in life, it will burden her soul in death; But oh, thrice guilty is he who drove her to the desperation which impelled her to the crime."[5] In a letter to Julia Ward Howe in 1873, Stanton wrote, "When we consider that women are treated as property, it is degrading to women that we should treat our children as property to be disposed of as we see fit."[6] These committed women put their money where their pens were by refusing ads for abortifacients.

The modern-day successors to Anthony and Stanton are Feminists for Life (FFL), an organization determined to reclaim the legacy of America's earliest women's rights activists, but "Debunking the myth that nineteenth-century women's rights supported abortion is a constant challenge, especially for historians faced with prejudice and political correctness."[7]

These pro-life women celebrate the early feminists' delight in motherhood. "Against society's norms, [Stanton] went out visibly pregnant and raised a flag to commemorate the birth of each of her [seven] children. She saw the beauty in women's awesome life-giving abilities and celebrated each new life publicly. . . . Stanton's views on the individuality of every human life . . . underscore for me the need to help women appreciate their unique abilities and fight against being molded into the wombless model of success society has foisted upon us," writes one feminist for life.[8]

Sarah Norton argued successfully for the admission of women to Cornell University. Norton wrote in 1870, "Child murderers practice their profession without hindrance, and open infant butcheries unquestioned. . . . Is there no remedy for all this antenatal child murder? . . . Perhaps there will come a time when the right of the unborn will not be denied or interfered with." The feminists who claim Norton's legacy work feverishly to see that the time she longed for is never realized.

The childless Susan B. Anthony responded to a man who told her he thought she would make a wonderful mother by explaining, ""I thank you, sir, for what I take to be the highest compliment, but sweeter even than to have had the joy of caring for children of my own has it been to me to help bring about a better state of things for mothers generally, so that their unborn little ones could not be willed away from them."[9] Today, a man who ventured such a compliment to one of Anthony's purported successors would be pilloried as a patriarchal supremacist, while Alice Paul, Anthony, and Stanton would see modern feminists as betraying women in the service of irresponsible men.

Mary Ann Glendon, the Learned Hand Professor of Law at Harvard University, explains that early feminists fighting for women's rights saw that "the ready availability of abortion would facilitate the sexual exploitation of women." They "regarded free love, abortion, and easy divorce as disastrous for women and children." What made the feminism of the 1970s so different, according to Glendon, was "a puzzling combination of two things that do not ordinarily go together: anger against men and promiscuity; man-hating and man-chasing."[10]

It is Serrin Foster, the dynamic president of Feminists for Life (FFL) since 1994, who is faithful to the legacy of America's earlier women's movement. She asks, "If women were fighting for the right not to be considered property, what gives them the right to consider their baby property?" Recognizing that 20 percent of all abortions are performed on college students, Foster launched FFL's College Outreach Program to provide practical resources for pregnant and parenting students and keeps up a grueling schedule traveling to campuses, where she's remarkably successful in changing students' minds about abortion. Planned Parenthood called FFL's "Question Abortion" campaign "the newest and most challenging concept in anti-choice student organizing."

Foster sharply criticizes colleges for providing abortions but no other services for pregnant students. "What kind of a choice is that?" she asks. She challenges abortion supporters and pro-lifers to work together to provide real alternatives to women facing crisis pregnancies.

Patricia Heaton, who plays Raymond's wife on the hit series *Everybody Loves Raymond*, is an FFL celebrity spokesman who loves Serrin Foster. She explains that "opponents think [our] group is strong and powerful, because Serrin is strong and powerful. She's the embodiment of what we feel about women. To think that the only thing a woman can do with a child is abort is demeaning to women and undermines everything that the women's movement has been working on since the suffragettes."[11]

Under the banner "Women Deserve Better," Patricia Heaton appears in one of FFL's print ad campaigns that reads: "Every 38 seconds in America a woman lays her body down, feeling forced to choose abortion out of a lack of practical resources and emotional support. Abortion is a reflection that society has failed women. There is a better way."

A Washington, D.C., native and graduate of Old Dominion University in Virginia, Foster previously worked at St. Jude's Children's Research Hospital and was director of development for the National Alliance for the Mentally Ill. Her current work is an extension of those earlier jobs as she devotes herself to the well-being of pregnant women and their unborn children.

In another refutation of the feminists' assertion that women overwhelmingly support their abortion agenda, a group of pro-life women formed the Susan B. Anthony List a dozen years ago to train and support pro-life activists and candidates. In 2003, the list had over 96,000 members and heading into an election year had raised over $2 million. They are vastly outspent by pro-abortion groups, but in the 2002 election cycle over 70 percent of the candidates the Susan B. Anthony List supported won their races for open seats. Only about a third of candidates in these races supported by Emily's List (the abortion-rights PAC), NARAL, or NOW won their races.

PLANNED PARENTHOOD'S BAD MOTHER

Just as the fiercely held pro-life views of early feminists are fiercely ignored by feminist academics and activists, Margaret Sanger's strong support for eugenics and contempt for family life are denied or dismissed.

Margaret Sanger is widely credited with being, perversely, the mother of Planned Parenthood. The famous crusader for birth control, whose views were also antithetical to the suffragettes', was its honorary chairman at its founding and remains a prized inspiration for its agenda. Gloria Feldt of Planned Parenthood declares, "I stand by Margaret Sanger's side," proudly leading "the organization that carries on Sanger's legacy."[12] Feldt promotes an airbrushed version of Sanger's cause. "In the 1920s, Margaret Sanger lectured to audiences around the country about the need for birth control—for the health, welfare, and personal rights of women and children, and for global peace and prosperity."[13]

When ABC News had a ninety-minute special devoted to "100 Years of Great Women," Sanger was prominently celebrated. Barbara Walters noted that activist women in Sanger's day had to be "not only smart, but fearless." Jane Fonda, herself an honoree, eagerly joined in the uncritical praise: "Margaret Sanger would be way at the top if I had to choose the most important women of the twentieth century."[14]

Born in 1879, into a poor family of eleven children, Sanger became the "nation's first birth-control martyr" when she was jailed for handing out contraceptives in 1917.[15] Although she married and had three children, she allowed that family life wasn't her thing. She recognized herself as "no fit person for love or home or children or friends or anything which needs attention or consideration."[16] Abandoning her husband and children, Sanger embarked on a series of affairs and turned her attention and consideration to seeing that the unfit didn't procreate. Her modern-day defenders either deny her enthusiastic support for eugenics or dismiss her advocacy as a faddish interest widely shared by her fellow progressives at the time.

While it is true that Sanger had plenty of company, her odious views can't be dismissively compared to bobbing her hair or flaunting a cigarette. The odious views her acolytes persist in denying or ignoring are documented in public and private records.[17]

Sanger was "glad" that post–World War I immigration restrictions were "drastic" enough to improve "the quality of our population." She did worry about the "increasing race of morons" that had already made it to America. She was disgusted with welfare spending for the "maintenance and perpetuation of these undesirables." Sanger saw the "morons" she railed against as "human weeds." In 1923 she told the New York State Legislature that "The Jewish people and Italian families are filling the insane asylums" and "hospitals" and "feeble-minded institutions," and taxpayers shouldn't have to support the "multiplication of the unfit." She said the state should see it had the money "to spend on geniuses."[18]

Sanger estimated that "nearly one-half of the entire [U.S.] population will never develop mental capacity beyond the state of moron."[19] At one point she proposed a nationwide moratorium on childbirth for five years.[20]

But even Margaret Sanger's contempt for motherhood and family life didn't mean she favored abortion to reduce the number of undesirables. And Sanger didn't oppose abortion because it was illegal and dangerous, as Planned Parenthood now maintains. She called abortion "barbaric" and a "horror" and abortionists "Blood-sucking men with M.D. after their names who perform operations for the price of so-in-so." The result of their handiwork was "the killing of babies" and "an outrageous slaughter."[21] She apparently believed that even "morons'" children should be spared that fate.

THE RADICALISM OF *ROE* V. *WADE*

Pro-abortion feminists' lies aren't confined to the facts long ago. With the help of sympathetic journalists, they lie about the current state of the law to mask just how radical their abortion agenda is. Senator Dianne Feinstein dishonestly dismisses victories by pro-life

Republicans by accusing them of distorting the feminists' agenda. She claims the GOP has "been successful at painting the view of the pro-choice movement as abortion on demand—and nothing could be further from the truth."[22] The senator's claim couldn't be further from the truth.

Pro-abortion feminists cast opponents of *Roe* v. *Wade* as enemies of women's rights, unfit for either polite company or federal court appointments.

No other Supreme Court decision has been so misunderstood. With Justice Harry Blackmun writing for the majority, in 1973 the Supreme Court held that a woman had a constitutional right to abortion based on an implied right to privacy "emanating" from the Ninth and Fourteenth Amendments. It ruled that a fetus is not a person, but a "potential life."

The Court set up a trimester framework where the woman's right to privacy and the state's right to protect potential life shift during the course of the pregnancy. In the first trimester, a woman's privacy right is paramount and the state can't restrict abortion for any reason. During the second trimester, the state can regulate abortion only to protect a woman's health. During the third trimester, a state can regulate or prohibit abortion to protect the life of the unborn child, unless the woman's life or health is threatened by carrying the baby to term. Restrictive abortion laws in all fifty states were thereby abolished.

In a companion case, *Doe* v. *Bolton*, decided the same day, the Court rendered its trimester framework moot by adopting a definition of "health" that is so broad it permits abortion for virtually any reason. According to the Court, maternal health meant "all factors—physical, emotional, psychological, familial, and the woman's age—relevant to the well-being of the patient."[23]

If a woman cites emotional, family, or psychological concerns, the government can't prohibit an abortion. This is the abortion-on-demand feminists demand, but the public opposes. The two cases represent one of the most radical abortion policies in the world.

These decisions aren't radical enough for a current member of the Court. Justice Ruth Bader Ginsburg expressed regret that her late mother hadn't "lived in an age when daughters are cherished as much as sons," when she stood with President Clinton on the day he announced her nomination to the Supreme Court in 1993. She has sharply criticized its 1977 decisions denying funding for abortion. She saw the Court's refusal to compel states to pay for abortions for poor women as a "stunning curtailment" of women's rights.[24]

Since the decision, there have been over 40 million abortions in America. A quarter of unborn children are aborted. Although he initially saw the decision as upholding the right of doctors to practice without interference, by the time he retired from the Court, Justice Blackmun had adopted the feminists' line about the landmark decision he authored: "It's a step that had to be taken as we go down the road toward the full emancipation of women."[25]

A PRO-LIFE PUBLIC

For over thirty years, the plain words of *Roe* and *Doe* have been distorted by the media. On the thirtieth anniversary of the decisions, media polls reflected the ongoing disinformation campaign. CNN asked, "Do you favor the Supreme Court ruling that women have the right to an abortion during the first three months of their pregnancy?" *The Washington Post's* poll misrepresented the 1973 decisions in the same way. Feminists translate public support for *Roe v. Wade*, which is based on the public's misunderstanding of the case, to support for their abortion-on-demand agenda.

When they are on the wrong side of public opinion on abortion, where they have uncomfortably resided for the past dozen years, feminists typically ignore or deny the polls.

Faye Wattleton was president of Planned Parenthood for fourteen years. A beautiful black woman whose fawning media coverage included a fashion spread in *Vogue* magazine, she put an extremely attractive face on Margaret Sanger's legacy. She would wax eloquent about the America she preferred to see: "A country like Thailand has such broad acceptance of sexuality. Children play with condoms! They blow them up as balloons" in such a pleasing contrast to "our kind of repressed, uptight attitude."

It was Wattleton who decided that Planned Parenthood should be in the lead in promoting abortion rights. When she led a demagogic campaign against the confirmation of Robert Bork to the Supreme Court, she explained, "At some point, you really have to take the gloves off."[26]

But Wattleton was only willing to mix it up on her own carefully controlled terms. When an equally attractive and articulate pro-life black woman was willing to take her on—Kay James of the National Right to Life Committee—Faye Wattleton refused to make joint appearances with her. While black Americans make up 12 percent of the population, black women account for 36 percent of all abortions. They are twice as likely to have an abortion as white women.

Wattleton's reluctance to face a well-armed opponent is understandable. Kay James would have had the better of the argument, because the facts are on her side. In 2003, even a poll commissioned by Wattleton's new outfit, the Center for the Advancement of Women, found that 51 percent of women thought abortion either should not be allowed or should only be available in cases of rape or incest or to save the life of the mother. Another 17 percent thought abortion ought to be available but with stricter limits. Only 30 percent agreed with Faye Wattleton and her abortion allies, which was down 4 points from two years earlier. Of the top twelve priorities for women, keeping abortion legal was second to last, beating by one point the importance of increasing the number of girls who participate in organized sports. (The poll for the center was conducted by Princeton Survey Research Associates and is available at Advancewomen.org.)

A 1999 poll by another feminist outfit, the Center for Gender Equity, found a similar 53 percent of American women favor outlawing abortion or permitting it only for cases of rape, incest, or to save the life of the mother. In fact, men typically favor abortion more than women do.[27]

In a rare departure from its typically feminist-friendly coverage, in 2003 *The New York Times* reported on the growing number of young people with pro-life views. Their own polling found that among people from eighteen to twenty-nine, only 39 percent thought abortion should be generally available, down from 48 percent ten years earlier. One young pro-lifer explained, "Myself and my classmates have never known a world in which abortion wasn't legalized. We've realized that any one of us could have been aborted."[28] Another poll conducted the following year found 51 percent of eighteen- to twenty-nine-year-olds identified themselves as "pro-life."[29]

A 2004 Wirthlin Worldwide poll found that 61 percent of those polled said abortion is "almost always bad" for women. Polls consistently show that about half of the public would ban abortion with exceptions for rape, incest, or life of the mother, which would ban about 95 percent of abortions. Another quarter of the public would ban all but first-trimester abortions.[30]

When not ignoring the public opinion at odds with their abortion-on-demand agenda, feminists either claim phantom supporters or attribute the lack of support to ignorance or intimidation. Roselyn O'Connell, president of the National Women's Political Caucus, claims, "There are a lot more pro-choice Republican women than anyone believes. Why they're quiet, I don't know." According to Congresswoman Loretta Sanchez (D–CA), "The biggest problem is that people don't know what's happening," and Congresswoman Louise Slaughter (D–NY) sees a lot of scaredy-cats in office. "So many of my colleagues say they don't really believe in the anti-choice position, but they are afraid."[31]

Because less than a quarter of the public agrees with Kate Michelman, Gloria Steinem, Gloria Feldt, and their allies that abortion should be available at any time for any reason, pro-abortion activists fight to keep the issue in the courts, beyond the reach of the public's pro-life sentiments. When she left her top post at NARAL, Kate Michelman headed to the Democratic National Committee to run a program called Campaign to Save the Court. But here too, pro-abortion feminists are at odds with public opinion.

A 2005 poll by Ayres, McHenry and Associates found that 79 percent of voters disagreed that a pro-life judicial nominee should be disqualified from serving on the Supreme Court.

Ellen Goodman recognizes the threat that public opinion poses to the *Roe* regime. Writing in 1989, when support for abortion was stronger than it is today, she warned that if a more conservative court "allows more restrictions, then access to abortion will hinge on public attitudes. It will be decided by Americans who are now ambivalent [sic] about the values that infuse this stalemated debate."[32]

Goodman was prescient. Elected officials haven't been kind to the abortion-rights agenda in recent years. Kate Michelman notes, "Since 1995, states have enacted nearly 400 restrictions on a woman's right to choose."[33] Gloria Feldt would much prefer that the fate of her agenda be in the hands of appointed judges with lifetime tenure. She laments that the White House and both chambers of Congress are controlled by "anti-choice politicians." So too are the majority of governorships, and "the state legislatures are overwhelmingly anti-choice."[34] These abortion absolutists seem to believe that some strange alchemy has handed such a political advantage to pro-life politicians given their constant claims that their abortion-on-demand agenda enjoys the broad support of voters.

When the question has been asked of voters, polls show the pro-life advantage is unequivocal in the voting booth. A 1996 Wirthlin exit poll found that among voters who listed abortion as one of their top two issues 45 percent voted for Bob Dole and 35 percent for Bill Clinton. A *Los Angeles Times* poll found even a bigger advantage for Dole among women who voted on the abortion issue. In 1994, among single-issue abortion voters, the pro-life advantage was 2 to 1.[35]

Former governor Christie Todd Whitman enjoys an undeserved reputation as an electoral powerhouse. This ardent supporter of abortion rights declared the anniversary of *Roe* v. *Wade* as New Jersey's "Day of Choice." In both her challenge and her reelection races she won with less than 50 percent of the vote. She failed to carry the majority of women voters in either race.

Following the election in November 2004, Kristin Day, the executive director of Democrats for Life of America, explained how her party had been damaged by abortion rights forces. She stated, "For the past 25 years, pro-life Democrats have been leaving the party over the issue of abortion." Day pointed out that twenty-five years ago, when Democrats held a 292-seat majority in the House, 125 of those seats were held by pro-life Democrats. As proof of a party establishment out of touch with the rank and file, she cited a June 2004 CBS poll that found "almost twice as many Democratic delegates as Democratic voters think abortion should be permitted in all cases."[36]

Before there was Kristin Day sounding a warning against the feminist sirens calling Democrats to join them on the radical fringes on abortion, there was former Pennsylvania governor Robert Casey.

The popular governor was barred from speaking at the 1992 Democratic convention owing to his pro-life views. In 1996, he wrote, "The truth is that *Roe* has failed to deliver. Failed to lift women out of poverty, failed to curb domestic abuse and violence against women. . . . The cruel irony is that abortion rights have underwritten the cynical and chauvinistic exploitation of women by predatory men, who so often abandon them. That is why, contrary to the abortion industry's spin doctors, most women in America oppose abortion on demand, while the most avid supporters of abortion are unmarried males between 18 and 35."[37]

Ten years later, when some Democrats urged the late governor's anti-abortion son, Robert Casey Jr., to run for the Senate in 2006, Kate Michelman expressed the feminists' anger. "It is a problem when leading Democrats publicly recruit candidates who do not share the core values of the party," she fumed, before likening pro-lifers to segregationists by comparing opposition to *Roe* v. *Wade* to opposition to *Brown* v. *Board of Education*.[38] Feminist Majority Foundation president Eleanor Smeal, joined by NOW president Kim Gandy, Gloria Steinem, and Faye Wattleton, sounded the alarm about a Bob Casey Jr. candidacy in an urgent e-mail, calling "feminists and progressives" to arms because "We deserve better than this. It will do women no good if both major parties are hostile to women's candidates and women's rights." Democrats had to "know that women will no longer be taken for granted."[39]

ABORTION ABSOLUTISTS

Feminists' unyielding support for this "women's issue" that doesn't have the support of women puts them at odds with the large majority of Americans who support recent protections for unborn children, like the ban on partial-birth abortions. Any measure that recognizes the humanity of an unborn child threatens pro-abortion feminists.

In 2004, Congress overwhelmingly approved the Unborn Victims of Violence Act, referred to as Laci and Conner's Law, after Laci Peterson, who was eight months pregnant with a son when she was murdered. The law allowed anyone who injured a pregnant woman and her unborn child during the commission of a federal crime to be charged with two separate crimes, thereby recognizing the child as a separate victim. Over half the states have similar laws. NARAL declared the law "a sneak attack on a woman's right to choose."

Under a proposal aimed at providing abortions as humanely as possible, a woman twenty or more weeks into pregnancy would have to be informed about the scientific evidence that fetuses at that stage of development feel pain. Her doctor would have to offer anesthesia for the fetus. A survey found that 78 percent of women and 75 percent of men approved of the proposal. Gloria Feldt objects to providing this information to women so the humane treatment accorded to animals being destroyed can be accorded to a little human. She accuses those concerned about fetal pain of "trying to elevate the status of the fetus above that of the woman." Any measure that makes clear that there is a young life involved in the call for "reproductive freedom" threatens Feldt's abortion agenda.

There are over four thousand pro-life crisis pregnancy centers nationwide, largely staffed by volunteers, that offer free services to women. That some of these centers offer free sonograms for their clients angered an abortion provider, who told *The New York Times*, "The bottom line is no woman is going to want an abortion after she sees a sonogram." In response, a director of one crisis pregnancy center explained, "For an abortionist to counsel a woman about fetal development, abortion risks, and support available to her should she want to carry the baby to term—they'd put themselves out of business."[40] The abortion industry makes an estimated $500 million a year.

Post-abortion groups, like Rachel's Vineyard, that provide support for women who have had abortions acknowledge that these women often need counseling and support—even healing. Planned Parenthood has no interest in the needs of women whose experiences indicate that there can be more than one victim of abortion.

Feminists vehemently defend the hideous procedure its opponents descriptively call "partial-birth abortion." A federal judge considering the constitutionality of a ban on the procedure described it as a "gruesome, brutal, barbaric, and uncivilized medical procedure—the fetus's arms and legs have been delivered outside the uterus while the fetus is still alive. With the fetus's head lodged in the cervix, the physician punctures the skull with scissors or crushes the head with forceps."[41]

In a rare instance of honesty, a leading member of the abortion rights movement broke ranks in 1997 to allow that abortion proponents had lied when they claimed that the partial-birth abortion procedure was extremely rare and used only to save the life or fertility of the mother. Ron Fitzsimmons, the executive director of the National Coalition of Abortion Providers, explained that he feared the truth about the procedure would damage the cause of abortion rights. He explained that, in truth, as many as five thousand of these abortions were performed each year and, "in the vast majority of cases," on "a healthy mother with a healthy fetus that is 20 weeks or more along."[42] Later numbers from abortion-friendly outfits would confirm that there were more partial-birth abortions being performed than abortion opponents claimed.[43]

President Clinton vetoed bans on partial-birth abortion that passed Congress with bipartisan majorities. In 1996, I had the pleasure of appearing as a guest on CNN's *Crossfire* with Eleanor Smeal, who was there to defend the indefensible. Her disdain for the facts was on full display as she stuck to the false story her ally Ron Fitzsimmons had also told when, as he later said, he "lied through my teeth" about the incidence of partial birth abortion.

The co-hosts asked us about the political fallout from the president's opposition to the ban. Catholic cardinals had demonstrated outside the White House in favor of outlawing the procedure. I cited polls showing that the public overwhelmingly supported the ban, and I called the procedure "four-fifths infanticide, one-fifth abortion." Smeal declared, "I've been studying the Catholic women's vote and where they are on issues like abortion. They are overwhelmingly pro-choice." I pointed out that seventy-two House Democrats voted for the ban, including Majority Leader Dick Gephardt, and that 64 percent of people who call themselves "pro-choice" supported the ban, which included an exception if the life of the mother was in jeopardy.

When the host on the right, Bob Novak, stated that 71 percent of the public supports the ban, Smeal countered that it wouldn't be the case "if you have the women who have had to have them, if they could hear those stories—" I interrupted (it was *Crossfire*, after all) to point out: "Dick Gephardt heard them. He wasn't dissuaded."

Smeal warned that the gender gap threatened anyone who doesn't allow this gruesome procedure, and I pointed out that 64 percent of women supported the ban. Bob Novak noted that people don't like abortion, and Eleanor Smeal responded, "For some women it saves their lives."[44]

What is telling about my experience in that debate with Eleanor Smeal is that these abortion absolutists don't openly defend their radical agenda. On the show, I freely admitted that I opposed both the partial-birth abortion procedure and other methods of abortion.

Just as Smeal was only willing to defend a procedure as allegedly life-saving for the mother, in an editorial urging the election of John Kerry, Kate Michelman also deceptively avoided making the case for abortion on demand. "If you are raped, if you are a victim of incest or if carrying a pregnancy to term will endanger your health, it's a decision for you—not the government—to make."[45] In the interest of accuracy, she might have added, "If you decide on the eve of your full-term delivery that you want to choose an abortion instead, it's your decision and not the government's."

Rather than forthrightly defend their abortion-on-demand agenda, these feminists make hysterical claims about the consequences of overturning *Roe* v. *Wade*. Kate Michelman likens the threat posed by the pro-life Bush administration "to the situation a few years ago in Romania, when government leaders required women workers to publicly post their menstrual cycles." Gloria Feldt maintains that without *Roe* v. *Wade* the country wouldn't just go back to 1972, when states had the authority to regulate abortion, but would rocket back to the 1950s. "Why are ["religious fundamentalists"] so eager to take us back to the stifling culture of the 1950s?" Feldt then recalls the days of racial segregation and poll taxes when women were denied credit cards and confined to "help wanted female" jobs.[46]

In fact, these feminists defend every single one of the over 40 million "choices" that have been made since *Roe* v. *Wade*, which itself was the product of a series of lies. Feminists at the time argued that they wanted to see "therapeutic" abortions legalized. The plaintiff in *Roe* falsely claimed she had been raped. Justice Blackmun falsely claimed that abortion had never been a common-law crime. He claimed to rest the wholly new right to abortion throughout nine months of pregnancy on the right to privacy he found lurking in the Constitution, but his daughter admits "that having three daughters and an outspoken, independent wife influenced his views about the choices women should be able to make in their lives."[47]

Feminists still lie about the incidence of back-alley abortions that served as a justification for legalization. In a celebratory column welcoming the upcoming euphemistically titled March for Women's Lives, in the spring of 2004, Ellen Goodman wrote, "After all, those of us who remember when birth control was illegal and when ten thousand American women a year died from illegal abortions don't have to imagine a world without choices."[48] As she later had to allow, her memory was faulty. When her column prompted charges that she was repeating "propaganda" or an "urban legend," she did a little research and admitted in a later column that the claim that there were thousands of deaths in the years prior to abortion's legalization (which she hadn't bothered to check in the thirty years since *Roe* v. *Wade*) is false.

In 1972, the year before *Roe* v. *Wade*, according to the federal Centers for Disease Control and Prevention, 39 women died of illegal or self-induced abortions. Overall improvements in prenatal and obstetrical care beginning in the 1940s saw the rate of pregnancy-related deaths from causes other than abortion drop at roughly the same rate as abortion-related deaths.

In a show of political muscle, hundreds of thousands joined the March for Women's Lives in April 2004. The crowds were thrilled when their feminist icons like Gloria Steinem, Patricia Ireland, and Kate Michelman were joined by Hollywood activists including Cybill Shepherd, Ashley Judd, and Whoopi Goldberg, who waved around a coat hanger at the rally. The marchers' political sentiments were represented with signs like IF ONLY BARBARA BUSH HAD A CHOICE, and STOP BUSH'S WAR ON WOMEN. The irony-impaired Congresswoman Maxine Waters (D–CA) explained, "I have to march because my mother could not have an abortion."

Another group of women was denied a permit to demonstrate on behalf of their convictions because they are the kind of women whose lives the March for Women's Lives prefers to censor. The Silent No More coalition represents women who regret their abortions. At the march, they would remain silent. One woman in the group, who had an abortion in 1971, said, "I'm hoping women might see our signs and be touched by them."

Actress and former Cover Girl model Jennifer O'Neill belongs to the coalition. "Choosing abortion is not empowering for women, rather it's the ultimate form of exploitation," O'Neill says, having had an abortion in the early 1970s. She explains that those who truly care about women are asking about the needs of pregnant women, "not protecting the business of abortion."

Elizabeth Fox-Genovese is the Eleonore Raoul Professor of the Humanities and professor of history at Emory University. This founding director of the university's Institute for Women's Studies also believes that the abortion rights agenda betrays women. She writes, "Doubtless we would benefit from more complete studies, but we now have enough evidence to say with confidence that for the vast majority of women, abortion represents a worst-case scenario—and, too often, a confirmation of their abandonment by the father of the child and by the larger community. More often than not, girls and women have abortions because they lack the support to have their child."[49]

Professor Fox-Genovese recognizes that "The pro-abortionists' embrace of women's right to the anxious freedom of disconnected individualism has effectively deprived women of the protections and support that pregnancy and maternity require."[50]

Kate Michelman, Faye Wattleton, Gloria Steinem, Gloria Feldt, Eleanor Smeal, and their abortion allies have been promoting an antiwomen agenda in the name of women's liberation by waging a campaign for "choice" on behalf of women who often feel they have no choice at all.

Conclusion | Mother Nature Is a Bitch

When Harvard president Larry Summers dared to suggest that perhaps sex differences played a role in the underrepresentation of women in some scientific fields, MIT professor Nancy Hopkins explained that if she hadn't fled from the presentation, "I would've either blacked out or thrown up." She told reporters, "When he started talking about innate differences in aptitude between men and women, I just couldn't breathe because this kind of bias makes me physically ill," thereby exhibiting an innate difference between men and some women when they hear something they find unpleasant.[1]

Dogmatic feminists like Hopkins insist that any discrepancy between the sexes in occupations or avocations is the result of discrimination. Evidence that the sexes are innately different threatens the androgynous agenda that launched the sexual revolution, the regulatory schemes that demand sex preferences, the denigration of motherhood, and the demand that women serve in combat. But in their battle to erase sex differences in every facet of modern life, feminists have squared off against Mother Nature, and she's no feminist.

Gustav Le Bon would have been smugly satisfied to witness Professor Hopkins's emotional, irrational reaction to an academic discussion. A hundred years ago, he argued that female inferiority "was so obvious that no one can contest it for a minute."[2] An obstetrics textbook popular in Le Bon's day stated, "A woman has a head too small for intellect but just big enough for love."[3] In the nineteenth century, recognized differences between the sexes persuaded observers that women were an inferior version of the species and were wrongly used to deny talented women an equal opportunity to pursue their ambitions. Now, these undeniable differences explain why the unparalleled equal opportunity American women enjoy cannot reasonably be expected to achieve a sex-blind sameness in parental roles, or in academic interests and achievement, or in employment, sports, or sex. Acknowledging these innate sex differences can liberate women—from the feminist orthodoxy in conflict with their natural talents and desires.

Feminists pointedly talk about "gender roles" or "gender identities" because they militantly insist that any differences are the result of oppressive cultural conditioning that can be changed. They represent the left-wing conviction that human beings are infinitely malleable. Professor Hopkins hysterically refuses to countenance any discussion of innate sex differences because any such hard-wiring dooms the ideological insistence that men and women are interchangeable.

One feminist academic bright light longs for the day when we can "transcend sexual gender," eliminate sex roles, and do away with the connection between sex and procreation so that "love relationships, and the sexual relationships developing out of them, would be based in the individual meshing together of androgynous human beings."[4] She has plenty of company in feminist academic circles who see a patriarchal plot in "compulsory heterosexuality." Professor Marilyn Frye of the University of Michigan explains, "A vital part of making generalized male dominance as close to inevitable as a human construction can be is the naturalization of female heterosexuality. Men have been creating ideologies and political practices which naturalize female heterosexuality continuously in every culture since the dawn of the patriarchies."[5]

On an ABC News special on sex differences in 1995, the high priestesses of feminism confronted their Galileo. Gloria Steinem made clear how opposed feminists are to free inquiry and debate when she declared, "It's really the remnant of anti-American, crazy thinking to do this kind of research. It's what's keeping us down, not what's helping us." ABC's John Stossel asked her, "Aren't women, in general, better nurturers?" and Steinem retorted, "No. Next question." Feminist lawyer Gloria Allred was equally uninterested in even discussing the topic. "This is harmful and damaging to our daughters' lives and to our mothers' lives, and I'm very angry about it"—an unreliable gauge of a topic's controversy to be sure, given Allred's natural agitated state. The feminists presented a united front in the face of compelling evidence about real differences between boys and girls.

An expert on the toy industry explained, "Toy marketers have tried over and over. They'd make twice as much money if every toy was bought by girls and boys, but the kids aren't buying it." Bella Abzug called talk of biological differences "a lot of poppycock" and announced that if the culture weren't sexist, little boys would happily play with dolls.

Stossel asked me to talk about the effect of lawsuits that forced fire departments to water down their physical standards in order to accommodate women. I saw, rather reasonably I thought, the end of the "firemen's carry," and explained that we could now look forward to being dragged down the steps of a burning building by the ankles, with our head hitting each step along the way. But Gloria Steinem was ready for me. "It's better to drag them out, because there's less smoke down there. I mean, we're probably killing people by carrying them out at that height, you know, so—I mean, you know, we need to look sensibly here at these jobs and what they really require, and not just some idea of what macho is." Desperate creativity must be a female trait.[6]

A female neuropsychiatrist engaged in sex-differences research explains, "I have been asked, even by women studying for their M.D.-Ph.D.'s, to stop our research or at least stop publicizing it. They are afraid that women will lose twenty years of gains if word gets out that the sexes aren't the same. I disagree. I think of the differences between male and female brains not in terms of strength or weakness but as something that is important to recognize."[7]

When feminist psychologist Alice Eagly began her career in gender research in 1975, she assumed that findings about the similarities between the sexes would bolster the case for equality. "It didn't work out," she explained. Twenty years and thousands of studies later, the Northwestern University professor concluded that there's truth in those dreaded sex stereotypes. She recognizes that men are, on average, more aggressive and enjoy superior math skills, and women are, on average, more nurturing, with better verbal skills. She also recognizes that her conclusions are unwelcome: "Mere research findings rarely displace an entrenched consensus," she says.[8]

Bernice Lott, now a professor emerita of psychology at the University of Rhode Island (URI), is part of that entrenched consensus threatened by the research findings. She objected to attention to sex differences because "it serves a primarily political function, as it serves to rationalize and perpetuate differences in power. . . . Such differences make media headlines because they justify the status quo and help maintain the continuing social and political barriers to gender equality."[9]

Lott's own research on the "female experience" was an inspiration for URI's decision to become one of the first universities in the country to offer a women's studies course in 1971. "We were ready and eager to breathe some new life into a discipline [psychology] that ignored half the population."[10] In turn, Lott and her protégées would ignore any unpleasant scholarship. Professor Eagly explains that most psychological textbooks minimize sex differences because their authors "are reluctant to say anything that might bring offense."[11]

The evidence feminists are determined to ignore increases with every year, and Professor Eagly has plenty of company among scientists and psychologists. Their fascinating and compelling research reaches utterly sensible conclusions readily visible to any eye not blinded by ideology. One expert on sex differences at the University of California at Berkeley has a word to describe people who believe "society alone molds children into sex roles"—"childless."[12] A leading female researcher explains that it's not possible to still believe that the sexes would be identical if the environment were right because, "We know too much to turn back."[13]

The field of evolutionary psychology offers cogent explanations for men and women's different traits and temperaments. Characteristics that boosted our early ancestors' chances for survival and reproduction were, naturally, inherited. "Evolutionary psychologists look to sexual selection to explain how male and female roles in reproduction and subsequently in the nurturing of the child would induce contrasting psychological predispositions in men and women," Professor Steven Rhoads of the University of Virginia explains in *Taking Sex Differences Seriously*.[14]

It is clear why evolution could be expected to produce different characteristics in men and women. All mammals' behavior displays sex differences. Specifically, "There are great rewards for males that show aggression toward other males, for males that seek mating opportunities, and for females that pay close attention to their babies." However, as human beings, our sexual division of labor is an unusual characteristic for mammals. Chimps all seek the same source of food, while in virtually all preagricultural societies, men sought food from mobile and unpredictable sources, while women, responsible for caring for children, sought food sources that were close and predictable.[15]

Imagine our early ancestors dwelling in a neighborhood of caves among treacherous enemies, two- and four-legged, in an inhospitable climate with food and water scarce. Now, translate their predictable behavior to your current neighborhood's hottest singles spot. An earlier "meat market" dictates modern behavior. "Women's minds evolved to suit the demands of bearing and rearing children and of gathering plant food. Men's minds evolved to suit the demands of rising in a male hierarchy, fighting over women and providing meat to the family."[16]

In their struggle to survive, men and women responded differently at the most elemental levels. The drive for reproductive success dictated the sexes' behavior. Men were anxious that they have lots of offspring to increase the number of heirs who might survive and so were interested in having plenty of sex. A woman had to be choosier. She would want some assurance that a mate could provide for her and protect her child. If she chose incorrectly, her child was doomed. He cared about youth and fertility and she cared about strength and status. Men were the aggressors, women wanted to make sure he would stick around. And humans have plenty of company in following this pattern. "Humanity shares this profile of ardent, polygamist males and coy, faithful females with about 99 percent of all animal species, including our closest relatives, the apes," according to Matt Ridley, the author of *Red Queen*.[17] After all, he notes, "In humans, the asymmetry is clear enough: nine months of pregnancy set against five minutes of fun."[18]

If a female cave-dweller subscribed to *Ms.* magazine and bought into being sexually liberated, evolution would have seen to it that her feminist genes would have perished along with her abandoned offspring.

Current surveys show that men care more about the attractiveness of a potential mate than women do, while women value resources in a mate twice as much as men do. Maureen Dowd angrily howls at the moon over the unfairness of it all. Although the different sex priorities in choosing a partner have been true across cultures, throughout recorded history, after speaking to a beautiful, successful actress friend who lamented that she was unmarried at age forty-six, Dowd announced, "I'd been noticing a trend along these lines, as famous and powerful men took up with the young women whose job it was to tend to them and care for them in some way: their secretaries, assistants, nannies, caterers, flight attendants, researchers, and fact-checkers." She might have added in angry frustration, "and not incredibly witty and powerful female columnists." Through her feminist lens, Dowd sees the men she condemns as demanding subservience from the young women they choose and ignores the biological urge to procreate that favors youthful fertility over fascinating banter with a menopausal actress or writer.[19]

And Maureen Dowd is living the lonely legacy of the sexual revolution. Powerful men are the biggest winners of libertine values that permit them to trade in the old model for a younger, prettier version and so enjoy the nubile years of more than one woman. Most divorced men find a new wife within three years, while a woman over age forty rarely remarries.[20]

Professor Rhoads cites a survey of college students who were asked to approach members of the opposite sex with a proposition, "I have been noticing you around campus. I find you very attractive.

Would you go to bed with me tonight?" Three quarters of the men said sure; none of the forty-eight women did. Similar studies have had similar results.[21] Charles Darwin recognized that the course of evolution was, to a large extent, in the hands of women when he wrote, "The power to charm the female has sometimes been more important than the power to conquer other males in battle."[22]

Even though they are swimming in a sea of gender equality, have been carefully schooled with role models of powerful assertive women, and are bombarded with advertising messages about flouting convention, when it comes to successful courtship modern young women are every bit as traditional as their benighted grandmothers. The sexual revolution is clearly at war with female psychology. "In 1952, 76 percent of the married couples polled said that the husband had proposed marriage; 12 percent said the wife had. In 1997, 82 percent said the husband proposed and 9 percent said the wife did. In this 1997 survey, couples under thirty proved to be the most traditional of all: 90 percent said the husband proposed and 4 percent said the wife did."[23]

For the feminist project, women's equality depends on their sexual liberation. Romantic love and emotional commitment represent dependency. Modern sex educators and popular textbooks preach sexual liberation for young women as the way to free them from patriarchal gender roles. "[G]ender textbooks say that socially constructed stereotypes—'sexual scripts'—are still entrenched despite the sexual revolution and still serve to explain the sexuality differences we see around us," Rhoads explains. He cites popular feminist authors who peddle the "Sex is about enjoying ourselves. 'Let's get on with it'" creed to women.[24] A typical women's studies textbook asserts, "The feminist movement has inspired among us a new openness about women's and men's sexuality and has helped free women's sexual behavior from its traditional constraints."[25] The misery attendant to the loosening of those traditional constraints, even when personally experienced, hasn't dampened the enthusiasm of younger feminists for sexual liberation.

Modern college life is marked by young men and women "hooking up" to have sex. Not only is there no romance, there's no relationship. Dr. Drew Pinsky observes that both participants in these impersonal couplings are typically at least partly drunk, but for very different reasons. The boys drink in order to relax and slow down their sexual response, the girls get drunk because "it numbs the experience for them, making it less embarrassing and less emotionally painful."[26]

About 11 percent of people between the ages of fifteen and twenty-four are infected with genital herpes, and about 33 percent of young women in the age group are thought to be infected with human papillomavirus (HPV). About 60 percent of gonorrhea cases and 74 percent of reported chlamydia cases in 2000 occurred in this age group.[27]

Rebecca Walker has an impeccable feminist lineage. She is the "biracial, bicultural and bisexual" daughter of Pulitzer Prize–winning novelist Alice Walker of *The Color Purple* fame and the goddaughter of Gloria Steinem. She graduated from Yale in 1992, and within a few years *Time* magazine named Walker as one of the nation's top fifty future leaders. She founded a nonprofit organization to better help young women to relate to the "third wave" of feminism. In 1996, she served on the national steering committee of Youth for Clinton/Gore '96, along with other young liberal activists, like actress Sarah Jessica Parker. Walker shares the enthusiasm of Parker's character Carrie Bradshaw and her pals on *Sex and the City* for carefree, casual sexual liaisons.

In a collection of essays for younger feminists, Walker recounted her own first sexual experience at age eleven, and offers this advice for the younger sisterhood: "It is obvious that the suppression of sexual agency and exploration, from within or from

without, is often used as a method of social control and domina-
tion."[28] Walker recounts that she had an abortion when she was
fourteen, and in her 2000 memoir, *Black, White & Jewish: Autobiography
of a Shifting Self*, she recounts being in the sixth grade and sharing sex
stories with a girlfriend while lamenting her mother's lack of interest in her safety. She is a child of divorce and writes, "I want her to
tell me that I can't go so far away from her while I'm so young, I
can't get on the 44 [bus] late at night and ride to the other side of
San Francisco to spend the night with people she doesn't know,
with people she's never seen."[29]

Young women who follow *Sex and the City*'s liberating advice
haven't been liberated from their female psyches. A Kaiser Family
Foundation survey in 2003 found that more than 60 percent of girls
who had sex wished they had waited. Another 2003 survey for the
National Campaign to Prevent Teen Pregnancy similarly found that
nearly 80 percent of sexually active teenage girls reported they
wished they had waited to have sex.[30] A female psychologist in
New York reports, "I can't tell you how many girls come in who are
bereft about having had sex too soon."[31]

Boys are less likely than girls to say they regret early sexual encounters, but they disapprove of female promiscuity. In a survey
that listed sixty-seven characteristics, "American men 'regard infidelity as the least desirable characteristic in a wife.'"[32] A husband's
infidelity doesn't threaten his wife's reproductive investment, while
her promiscuity risks his investment in a child that is not his own.

This much-decried double standard has ancient precedents.
Men anxious for their own progeny had little interest in providing
for another cave dweller's offspring, and only a faithful sexual partner ensured that the children he provided for were his own. For
women, a caring partner seems to be an aphrodisiac. A comprehensive survey found that women in committed relationships, either

married or living with a partner, reported more frequent and better sex than uncommitted singles of every age.[33]

The most popular sex manual in 1876 recognized what eludes modern feminists. *The Relations of the Sexes* explained, "[W]omen are not like men in sensual matters. They—most of them at least—do not love lust for lust's sake. Passion must come to them accompanied not only with love, but with the tender graces of kindness and consideration."[34] After a comprehensive discussion of both the animal kingdom and human societies throughout the ages, Matt Ridley summarizes some "universal features." Women seek monogamy even when polygamy is allowed, and they don't look for sexual variety for its own sake. "The temptress interested in a one-night stand with a man whose name she does not know is a fantasy fed by male pornography," he explains. "Lesbians, free of constraints imposed by male nature, do not suddenly indulge in sexual promiscuity; on the contrary, they are remarkably monogamous. None of this is surprising: Female animals gain little from sexual opportunism, for their reproductive ability is limited not by how many males they mate with but how long it takes to bear offspring. In this respect men and women are very different."[35]

Mother Nature predicts the destructive consequences of the sexual revolution and has lots to say about the rest of the feminist agenda of androgyny. Rebecca Walker's anthology on feminism is a standard text in women's studies courses, and she frequently lectures at events like San Jose's 2004 Girls for a Change Summit, which invited girls in grades 6 to 12 to the convention center to hear her liberated views. She is raising a son with another woman and has turned her attention to men in the hope of liberating them, too, from our oppressive culture. Walker has edited another anthology, *What Makes a Man: 22 Writers Imagine the Future*, that seeks to unteach the "cultural lessons" that allegedly leave men hurt and confused.

She explains that just as women were once in pain and unable to realize their potential, "men are similarly hampered by this masculine ideal, in which they are expected to repress their emotions." She disapproves of her own son engaging in sports and thinks "it's a cop-out to say that boys are biologically determined to be aggressors."[36]

Rebecca Walker may have been too busy lecturing and writing about culturally determined gender roles to pay close attention to the real-world behavior of that little boy in her home. And she wouldn't have had to wait too long to observe innate behaviors. Studies indicate that sex differences are obvious within hours of birth.

On the first day of life, girls are more drawn to a picture of a face, and newborn boys to a mechanical mobile. At a year, boys have shown a stronger preference for a video of cars, while girls at age one prefer a talking head. In a study of stories told by two-year-olds, people were the subject of the great majority of stories by girls, but a small minority of stories told by boys. Researchers conclude that girls are hard-wired to be more people-centered than boys.[37]

While our male ancestors were pursuing the solitary responsibility of finding game, and developing the spatial memory necessary to find their way home, their female mates were back at the caves building the social alliances that would help them survive. Women needed a community of other women to help with childbirth and child care. Women score far higher than men on reading facial expressions, on empathizing, and in language skills. "Women who had a talent for decoding their male partner's next move would have had a greater success in avoiding spousal aggression. Women who were good at detecting deception would have also been more skilled at finding sincere males to mate with, and at judging whether a man would treat them well or just impregnate them."[38]

Mothers are particularly good at reading babies' faces, a skill that would have been the result of natural selection because it boosted the chances of survival for preverbal babies. A study of 186 societies found that mothers, with their superior skills, are the exclusive or primary caretakers of infants.[39]

Girls talk earlier and more often than boys. They are better readers and spellers. More men stutter. Women's sentences are, on average, longer than men's, and they articulate words faster than men. "Females may have better language systems because their survival depended on a more empathetic, rapid, tactful, and strategic use of language."[40]

When very young children are asked what toys are appropriate for boys and which for girls, they are unable to answer. They don't know the gender stereotypes about trucks and dolls, but they know the sex-typical toys they like themselves. It seems that the toy preferences that so frustrate progressive parents predate the stereotypes that are blamed for the inability to get little Jane to ignore the baby doll and cradle in favor of a toy tractor. Ridley explains that when we give children the sex-specific toys they favor, "We are reinforcing the stereotypical obsessions that they already have, but we are not creating them."[41]

On that fateful day, Larry Summers shared a story about his toddler twin daughters, who were steered away from traditional toys only to be overheard saying, "Look, Daddy truck is carrying the baby truck." Lest his audience think that there was a problem in the Summers household that called for some feminist crisis intervention, Dr. Summers pointed out that there were stubborn sex differences in the "one hundred different kibbutzes" in Israel that tried mightily to raise children free of stereotypes.

When it comes to aggression, sex differences "appear by the second year of life, well before girls and boys are capable of reliably discriminating [between] the sexes or knowing which behaviors are more characteristic of one than the other."[42] According to experts who examined homicide records from the past seven hundred years over diverse cultures, "There is no known human society in which the level of lethal violence among women even approaches that among men." Historic data indicate that fully two thirds of male homicides arise from a social conflict over respect or status.[43] When they are in groups, boys quickly establish a hierarchy that they carefully monitor and maintain, while studies reveal girls prefer reciprocal friendships where relationships depend on communicating and nurturing.[44]

Evolutionary psychology, and biology—male and female chromosomes and hormones—combine to create the sex differences that frustrate the feminists' liberation agenda. Cambridge University professor Simon Baron-Cohen's thesis is that "the female brain is predominantly hard-wired for empathy. The male brain is predominantly hard-wired for understanding and building systems." This division produced evolutionary advantages for each sex.

Like most researchers who dare to venture into the political minefield in order to study essential sex differences, he takes pains to explain that his conclusions shouldn't be misinterpreted. For example, "not all men have the male brain, and not all women have the female brain," so individual men can be well suited for caring professions and some women are good fits for technical fields. And "looking for sex differences is not the same as stereotyping," which judges individuals based on an average, while science shows that people can fall outside the averages for their group.[45]

But the measurable biological differences between the sexes, on average, can tell us why the feminists' ideological campaign for rigid equality in every facet of American life is a misguided and impossible goal. Their gender theory, which holds that disparities between the sexes are the result of cultural conditioning and therefore subject to change, covers every facet of life. A recent example depicts the ongoing assault that refuses to accept even the most obvious sex differences. Flush with righteous anger over all discrepancies, and unable to give their radical ideology a rest, feminist academics see poisonous sexual politics in toilets. Really.

In 2005 Olga Gershenson of the University of Massachusetts at Amherst and Barbara Penner of University College in London invited contributions for the collection they were editing entitled *Toilet Papers: The Gendered Construction of Public Toilets*. This feminist scholarship "will work from the premise that public toilets, far from being banal or simply functional, are highly charged spaces, shaped by notions of propriety, hygiene and the *binary gender division*." They point out that "public toilets are among the very few openly segregated spaces in contemporary Western culture," and so "provide a fertile ground for critical work interrogating how conventional assumptions about the body, sexuality, privacy, and technology can be formed in public space and inscribed through design."[46]

If even the biological imperative to, ahem, either stand or sit is seen as an example of the repressive "gender division" and a result of "conventional assumptions" about sex differences, it's little wonder that feminists reject the convincing evidence about the less immediately obvious differences in male and female anatomy, beginning with the brain.

Feminists of an earlier day understandably felt threatened by the notion that there was a difference in intelligence between the sexes. In 1898, author Charlotte Perkins Gilman complained, "The brain is not an organ of sex. As well speak of the female liver." But modern science tells us that the female liver is "one of the most sexually distinctive of organs." And sex hormones don't stop at the neck.[47] Women's livers metabolize drugs differently and oxidize alcohol more slowly than a male liver. Maybe a woman getting tipsy on less liquor than a man of equal weight shows an evolutionary preference for "cheap dates."[48]

The differences continue. "The female immune system, ever vigilant, responds more vigorously to common infections, offering extra protection against viruses, bacteria, and parasites. This may explain why Mom is often the last one standing during a family flu siege."[49] Women take fewer breaths each minute, and have fewer sweat glands and red blood cells. They sleep more lightly and awake more easily. More men get hiccups.[50]

Women's brains weigh about 10 to 15 percent less than men's brains. This difference is relative to differences in overall body weight. Testing also shows other meaningful differences in our senses. Men are more sensitive to bright light, better detect differences in light, and can see better at long distances as they age. Women hear a broader range of sounds, and their hearing begins to deteriorate later in life.[51] Women have a better sense of smell; in infancy girls spend more time with scented rattles.[52] "When a male puts his mind to work, brain scans show neurons turning on in highly specific areas. When females set their minds on similar tasks, so many brain cells light up that their bright-colored scans glow like Las Vegas at night."[53]

"[N]euroscientists have determined that men have fewer neurons connecting the left and right hemispheres of the brain. This difference may help to explain why women are better at talking about their emotions. (The left brain controls talking; the right brain controls emotions)."[54] Men and women use different parts of their brains when they navigate. Generally, women use landmarks when giving directions; men offer directions in terms of north and south and the distance in miles.[55]

Four specific differences between the sexes stand out repeatedly in psychological tests. Girls perform verbal tasks better; boys are better at mathematical tasks. Boys are more aggressive and better at certain spatial tasks, like reading a map. Women judge character and moods better than men. Men needed spatial skills to hit moving targets and to make tools. Women's superior object and location memory helped them to find berries and plants.[56]

"[T]he mental differences between men and women are caused by genes that respond to testosterone." If men are exposed as embryos to less than the usual testosterone, they are effeminate and unassertive.[57] Likewise, girls exposed in utero to a hormone that acts like testosterone have some masculine traits. This condition, called congenital adrenal hyperplasia (CAH), permits studies of the effects of this testosterone-like substance on girls. Girls with CAH score higher on spatial tests than other girls, compete in athletics more often, and are more competitive.[58]

As they get older, girls with CAH are less interested in having children and more interested in "having a career versus staying at home" than most girls.[59] Studies of baby girls who are exposed to elevated levels of testosterone show effects similar to the CAH condition. A female twin born with a twin brother is more likely to enjoy taking risks and does better on spatial tests.[60] "High-testosterone women are more assertive, more career-oriented, and more likely to have high-status and traditionally male-dominated careers."[61]

The feminists' monolithic view of what women want and how they should behave might suit some of these high-testosterone women, but the hard-wiring of typical women argues against the sex-blind nirvana feminists seek.

Larry Summers also ventured the opinion that perhaps women professionals' family responsibilities were in conflict with the demands of an academic career. A Pew Research Center survey found that 86 percent of mothers rated their children a 10 for their importance as a source of happiness, on a scale of 1 to 10, while only 30 percent of employed women rate their job as a 10. Even unmarried, childless women rate personal relationships as more important to their happiness than jobs or hobbies.[62]

And innate abilities can be expected to dictate career choices that, in turn, dictate wages. The fields of metalworking, crafting musical instruments, and the construction industries are almost entirely male. This is true almost universally, even though physical strength is not always the key factor. These occupations do demand the typically male strength in constructing systems.[63]

It's not hard to appreciate that, on average, individuals with the female brain make excellent teachers, nurses, therapists, and social workers because these demand empathizing skills. The male brain, with its superior systemizing skills, makes for good scientists, engineers, architects, electricians, bankers, and toolmakers.[64] Predictably, people tend to enjoy what they are good at and so will make career choices based, in part, on these sex differences in abilities.

With respect to schooling, "sex differences in childhood are larger and more important than sex differences in adulthood."[65] There are differences between boys and girls in hearing, in the response to confrontation, and in developmental timetables. Girls and boys learn math differently and understand literature differently.[66] Dr. Leonard Sax concludes, "There are no differences in what girls and boys can learn. But there are big differences in the best ways to teach them."[67]

Boys and girls have different reading interests, but feminists have seen to it that these differences can't be accommodated without engaging in the dreaded gender stereotyping. While girls prefer stories about a character's behaviors and motives, boys want to read about strong male characters who take risks for noble ends. "War stories and books about struggles really resonate with boys," explains one expert. "They see life as a battle, and war stories appeal to that side of their nature."[68] Dr. Sax reports that in his practice "I'm seeing many boys who have never had the experience, not even once, of reading a book that really excites them." He concludes, "The first priority of schools must be education. Social engineering comes second."[69]

An appreciation of sex differences could be used to boost the academic achievement of boys and girls. Instead, schools are futilely attempting to wipe out these differences because in the view of influential feminists they represent an oppressive social construction. Feminists hysterically react to single-sex education as though apartheid were being introduced in our schools.

When the Bush administration proposed relaxing restrictions on single-sex public schools and classrooms, NOW president Kim Gandy fumed that such an educational option "perpetuates sex stereotypes and undermines workplace equality."[70]

Kim Gandy's ideological opposition ignores real contributions to the advancement of women. The Young Women's Leadership School in New York's Harlem, founded in 1996, sends 100 percent of its disadvantaged female students to college. NOW, together with the ACLU, has complained formally about the public high school.[71] Difference does not mean unequal, and the refusal to recognize differences that can have a fundamental effect on learning shortchanges girls and boys in the name of "equality."

The current Title IX regime that began life as an antidiscrimination law and is now enforced as a strict quota policy ignores the sex differences that show men are far more interested in sports than women. The feminist head of a Title IX consulting company asserts the tired dogma, "Women aren't born less interested in sports. Society conditions them."[72] Four times as many men as women are categorized as "strong sports fans," and far more men than women read the sports pages.[73] The Olympics do draw almost as many female viewers as male, but the president of NBC Sports highlights the differences in interest when he explains: "Men will sit through the Olympics for almost everything, as long as they get to see some winners and losers. . . . Women tend to approach this differently. They want to know who the athletes are, how they got there. . . . They want an attachment, a rooting interest."[74]

Boys' greater preference for physical competition starts early. "Studies from the 1920s to the 1990s show that in the preschool years, girls are more interested in dance, and boys in balls and rough-and-tumble play. These differences begin to appear before the age of two. By grade school the boys' games are more competitive, longer in duration, with more rules and interdependence between players and with clear winners and losers." A study of fourth and sixth graders showed that during free play, 50 percent of the time boys are competing with other boys, while girls engage in such competition only one percent of the time.[75]

Professor Baron-Cohen notes that males' greater interest in sports neatly matches their strength in systemizing. Sports fans combine a rule-based system, an organizable system (players and teams), and a statistical system.[76] As NBC Sports recognizes, as better empathizers, women want to know all about the ice skater who keeps an exhausting training schedule despite her mother's serious illness, or the brave gymnast who overcame his childhood disability.

Although the Title IX quota warriors have zero interest in the well-being of boys, it's additionally worth noting for the benefit of fair-minded policy makers that "boys need sports more than girls because boys have more difficulty than girls in making friends." Boys' friendships tend to be based on shared interests in the same activity, and competitive sports are a favorite endeavor.[77]

In addition to males' being bigger and stronger, their aggression, interest in competition, and natural affinity for hierarchies are characteristics important to success in the military. Male superiority in throwing accuracy is evident among two-year-olds. This is a welcome skill in the military, as is the ability to see movement in a camouflaged environment, which is another area where males excel.[78]

Baron-Cohen notes, "The good systemizer with slightly reduced empathy might be prepared to do what was necessary to win, even if this required the sacrifice of someone's feelings to make it possible. . . . Someone with a balanced brain might be a nicer person to have as a boss, but he or she might lack the ruthless edge needed to survive and prosper when the going gets tough."[79]

The sexes can be equal without being the same. Women and men each have their own strengths and skills in a grand design that allows us to complement each other as coworkers and coeds, as friends and lovers.

Harvard president Larry Summers was right. Feminists like Nancy Hopkins, Rebecca Walker, and Kim Gandy have to repeal the laws of nature to realize the kind of doctrinaire sexual equality they demand.

Women who make the world worse by denying the complementary roles of husband and wife and father and mother dismiss children's need for the example and attention of both parents. They have weakened the family and put children at risk. Women who make the world worse by encouraging careers at the expense of family seek to deny women the choices they freely make. Women who make the world worse by demanding that sex differences be eliminated in classrooms and on playing fields engage in a radical social engineering that harms young boys and girls alike. Women who make the world worse by insisting that American women engage in combat weaken the military and jeopardize lives. Women who make the world worse by holding candidates hostage to a phony gender gap have poisoned our politics. Women who make the world worse by lying about their radical abortion agenda betray women and their unborn children.

All of these women who make the world worse by waging a destructive war between the sexes are at war with Mother Nature.

Notes

1 | HOW RADICAL FEMINISTS HAVE WEAKENED THE FAMILY

1. Betty Friedan, *The Feminine Mystique*, W. W. Norton & Co., updated 1997, p. 381.
2. "Why Congress Should Ignore Radical Feminist Opposition to Marriage," The Heritage Foundation, Backgrounds. June 16, 2003, quoting Marlene Dixon, *Why Women's Liberation?: Racism and Male Supremacy.* San Francisco Bay Area Radical Education Project, 1969.
3. Robin Morgan, ed., *Sisterhood Is Powerful*, Random House, 1970, p. 537.
4. Germaine Greer, *The Female Eunuch*, McGraw Hill, 1971, p. 233.
5. Jessie Bernard, *The Future of Marriage*, World Publishing, 1972, p. 48.
6. Ibid., p. 51.

7. Bart Barnes, "Sociologist Jessie Bernard Dies; Wrote on Equality of the Sexes," *Washington Post*, October 10, 1996.

8. *The Family in America*, Volume 18, Number 2, February 2004, Rockford Institute, quoting Singer in "Staying Together," *Ladies Home Journal*, September 1991.

9. Betty Friedan, *The Second Stage*, Summit Books, 1981, p. 22.

10. Barbara Ehrenreich, "Oh, Those Family Values," *Time*, July 18, 1994.

11. Marylouise Oates, "Thomas Serves Up 'Free to Be' Family Style," *Los Angeles Times*, September 16, 1987.

12. Jennifer Harper, "Marriage Treated Harshly in Texts; Survey Gives an A to Only One of 20 Books Colleges Use," *Washington Times*, September 18, 1997.

13. Ibid.

14. John Leo, "Marriage Oppressive Institution, the Cultural Elite Is Still Attacking the Traditional Family," *Charleston Daily Mail*, September 17, 1997.

15. Footnotes, "Report Criticizes Textbooks on Marriage and Family Life," *Chronicle of Higher Education*, September 26, 1997.

16. Council on Families, *Closed Hearts, Closed Minds: The Textbook Story of Marriage*, Institute for American Values, 1997, p. 7.

17. Ana Veciana-Suarez, "Study Says College Texts Paint a Grim Picture of Marriage; Council on Families Report Finds Many Books Are Riddled with Errors," *Akron Beacon Journal*, October 7, 1997.

18. Karen S. Peterson, "Both Sexes Enjoy Feast of Marriage; Wedded Bliss Is Just as Good for Women," *USA Today*, October 3, 2000, p. 1D.

19. Amy M. Braverman, "Healthy, Wealthy, & Wed," *University of Chicago Magazine*, October 2003.

20. Peterson, "Both Sexes Enjoy Feast of Marriage."

21. Braverman, "Healthy, Wealthy & Wed."

22. Ibid.

23. Ibid.

24. Ibid.

25. Norval Glenn and David Blankenhorn, "Staying Together for the Kids," *Dallas Morning News*, January 18, 1998.

26. Rutgers University, "The State of Our Unions: The Social Health of Marriage in America," The National Marriage Project, 2003, p. 9.

27. Rutgers University, "The State of Our Unions," 2004.

28. Ibid.

29. "The Latest in the War on Marriage," *New York Post*, July 17, 1999.

30. Maggie Gallagher, "Shrinks Who Think Dads Stink: The War on Marriage Continues," *New York Post*, July 22, 1999.

31. Dr. Wade F. Horn, "Lunacy 101: The Need for Fathers Questioned," *Washington Times*, July 6, 1999.

32. Karl Zinsmeister, "Fatherhood Is Not for Wimps," *American Enterprise*, September 1, 1999.

33. Rutgers University, "The State of Our Unions," 2004.

34. Germaine Greer, "Editorial," *Daily Telegraph*, May 29, 2005.

35. Robert Rector, "Using Welfare Reform to Strengthen Marriage," *American Experiment Quarterly*, Summer 2001; Robert E. Rector and Kirk A. Johnson, "Understanding Poverty in America," Backgrounder, The Heritage Foundation, January 5, 2004.

36. National Fatherhood Initiative, "Father Facts," at Fatherhood.org.

37. Maggie Gallagher, *The Abolition of Marriage*, Regnery, 1996, p. 196.

38. U.S. Senate, Testimony before the Committee on Health, Education, Labor and Pensions, Subcommittee on Children and Families, April 29, 2004.

39. Council on Family Law, "The Future of Family Law: Law and the Marriage Crisis in North America," Institute for American Values, p. 17.

40. Wendy McElroy, "Congress Should Kill Discriminatory Domestic Violence Act," June 29, 2005, at ifeminists.com.

41. Ibid.

42. Cathy Young, *Ceasefire: Why Women and Men Must Join Forces to Achieve True Equality*, Free Press, 1999, p. 117.

43. Ibid., p. 114.

44. Ibid., pp. 99, 134.
45. Steven E. Rhoads, *Taking Sex Differences Seriously*, Encounter Books, 2004, p. 138.
46. Gallagher, *Abolition of Marriage*, p. 36.
47. Amy Driscoll, "After 2 Months of Ire, Feminist's Ex-husband Calls for a Cease-fire," *Miami Herald*, June 27, 2000.

2 | DAY CARE GOOD; MOTHER BAD

1. Betty Friedan, *The Feminine Mystique*, W. W. Norton & Co., 1963, p. 346.
2. Rhoads, *Taking Sex Differences Seriously*, p. 17.
3. www.americanoutlook.org/index.cfm?fuseaction=article_detail&id=1533
4. Claudia H. Deutsch, "Behind the Exodus of Executive Women: Boredom," *New York Times*, May 1, 2005.
5. George Gilder, *Men and Marriage*, Pelican, 1986, pp. 168–169.
6. "The Parent Trap," *New York Times*, January 4, 1998, p. 21.
7. Joan K. Peters, *When Mothers Work*, Da Capo Press, 1997, p. 4.
8. Ibid.
9. Ibid., p. 163.
10. Ibid., pp. 163–165. Note to readers who might be more concerned than Lily's mother was: Rosa returned, but who knows for how long. The book's credits thank Guadalupe Ramirez, "the babysitter who made this work possible and who has shared in the pleasure of raising our daughter." Apparently, Peters successfully "dispersed the mothering."
11. Peters, *When Mothers Work*, pp. 90, 199.
12. "Goodbye to Momism," *New York Times*, May 3, 1998.
13. Susan Chira, *A Mother's Place*, Harper Perennial, 1998, p. 73.
14. Ibid., pp. 188, 277.
15. Gretchen Ritter, "The Messages We Send When Moms Stay Home," *Austin American-Statesman*, July 6, 2004.

16. Neil Gilbert, "What Do Women Really Want?" *The Public Interest*, Number 158, Winter 2005, pp. 30–33.

17. Mackenzie Carpenter, "Santorum Book Stirs Debate on Child Care," *Pittsburgh Post-Gazette*, July 7, 2005, quoting Democratic pollsters Greenberg, Quinlan, Rosner Research, Inc.

18. Ritter, "The Messages We Send."

19. *Crossfire*, CNN, March 1, 1999.

20. Brian C. Robertson, *There's No Place Like Work: How Business, Government, and Our Obsession with Work Have Driven Parents from the Home*, Spence, 2000, p. 33.

21. Brian C. Robertson, *Day Care Deception*, Encounter Books, 2003, pp. 4–5.

22. Sylvia Ann Hewlett and Cornel West, *The War Against Parents*, Houghton Mifflin, 1998, p. 95.

23. Ibid., p. xviii.

24. Robertson, *Day Care Deception*, p. 31, quoting from Bernard Goldberg, *Bias: A CBS Insider Exposes How the Media Distort the News*, Regnery, pp. 163–78.

25. Robertson, *Day Care Deception*, p. 48.

26. Ibid., p. 55.

27. Ibid., p. 76.

28. Ibid., pp. 51–52.

29. www.americanoutlook.org/index.cfm?fuseaction=article_detail&id =3151

30. Robertson, *Day Care Deception*, p. 78.

31. "The Case for Staying Home," *Time*, March 22, 2004.

32. Robertson, *Day Care Deception*, p. 37.

33. Ibid.

34. Suzanne Venker, *7 Myths of Working Mothers: Why Children and (Most) Careers Just Don't Mix*, Spence, 2004, p. 43.

35. Daphne de Marneffe, *Maternal Desire: On Children, Love and the Inner Life*, Little, Brown, 2004, pp. 157, 178.

36. Ibid., p. 37.

37. Ibid., p. 8.
38. Ibid.
39. Ibid., p. 154.
40. Venker, 7 Myths of Working Mothers, pp. 5, 67.
41. Ibid., p. 122.
42. Ibid., p. 134.
43. Sylvia Ann Hewlett, *Creating a Life: What Every Woman Needs to Know About Having a Baby and a Career,* Miramax, 2003.
44. Phillip Longman, *The Empty Cradle: How Falling Birthrates Threaten World Prosperity and What to Do About It,* Basic Books, 2004, p. 83.
45. Peters, *When Mothers Work,* p. xiii.
46. Jennifer Roback Morse, "Why the Market Can't Raise Our Children for Us," *The American Enterprise,* May/June 1998.
47. Hewlett, *Creating a Life,* pp. 83–97.
48. Ibid., p. 92.
49. Ibid., p. 114.
50. Ibid., p. 3.
51. Ibid., pp. 84–87.
52. Ibid., p. 203.
53. Ibid., pp. 241–242.
54. Ibid., pp. 31–33.

3 | SKIRTING THE TRUTH—LIES ABOUT WAGES, DISCRIMINATION, AND HARASSMENT

1. *Today Show,* NBC, February 8, 2005.
2. Molly Ivins, "Pay-Gap Explanation Gets Thinner Each Year," *Tulsa World,* January 3, 2004.
3. Judy Mann, "Waiting for the Equal-Pay Ship to Dock," *Washington Post,* March 3, 1999.
4. Francine Knowles, "War of the Wages," *Chicago Sun-Times,* November 18, 1998.
5. Betsy Hart, "Women's Wages Are Fine, but Study Stinks," *Chicago Sun-Times,* February 10, 2002.

6. Ibid.
7. Judy Mann, "Pay Discrimination Is No Dirty Little Secret," *Washington Post,* June 15, 2001.
8. Sandra Sobieraj, "Clinton Calls for More Pay for Women," AP, January 30, 1999.
9. Rachel Smolkin, "Equality at Work Remains Elusive," *Pittsburgh Post-Gazette,* June 3, 2001.
10. Thomas Sowell, "Statistical Malpractice," *Washington Times,* July 24, 2004.
11. Sally Pipes, "Discrimination Suit Against Wal-Mart Obtains Class-Action Status," Pacific Research Institute, July 8, 2004, pacificresearch.org.
12. Steven Malanga, "Class Action? Third Aisle to the Left," *Wall Street Journal,* July 5, 2004.
13. cfif.org, December 9, 2004.
14. "Income Gap Seen for College-Educated White Women," *Boston Globe,* March 28, 2005.
15. Diana Furchtgott-Roth and Christine Stolba, *Women's Figures: An Illustrated Guide to the Economic Progress of Women in America,* AEI Press, 1999, p. 17.
16. Ibid., p. 15.
17. Kingsley R. Browne, *Biology at Work: Rethinking Sexual Equality,* Rutgers University Press, 2002, p. 7.
18. Mike Cleary, "Clinton Touts Equal Pay for Women," *Washington Post,* January 25, 2000.
19. Ibid., p. 18.
20. The Family in America, New Research, The Howard Center, Rockford, Illinois, citing a study in *Journal of Marriage and Family,* June 2003.
21. Warren Farrell, *Why Men Earn More,* Amacom, 2005, pp. xviii, xix.
22. Ibid., p. xxi.
23. Ibid., p. xxxii.
24. Ibid., p. 12.
25. Ibid., p. 15.

26. Ibid., p. 20.

27. Ibid., p. 72.

28. Ibid.

29. Browne, *Biology at Work*, p. 64.

30. Farrell, *Why Men Earn More*, p. 136.

31. Browne, *Biology at Work*, p. 75.

32. Ibid., p. 83.

33. *Washington Post*, February 27, 2005.

34. Farrell, *Why Men Earn More*, pp. 46–47.

35. Ibid., p. 31.

36. Ibid., p. xxix.

37. Ibid., p. 63.

38. Ibid., pp. 82, 85, 89.

39. Ibid., p. 136.

40. Charles S. Clark, "Haggling over Sexual Harassment," *St. Louis Post-Dispatch*, October 10, 1991.

41. John Aloysius Farrell, "Rewriting the Rules," *Boston Globe Magazine*, February 7, 1999.

42. Ibid.

43. Eugene Volokh, "A National Speech Code Courtesy of the EEOC," *Chicago Tribune*, September 14, 1997.

44. Ibid.

45. Cal Thomas, "Feminists Complicit in Rape in America," *Austin American-Statesman*, February 27, 1999.

46. R. D. Pohl, "Adrienne Rich's Journey from Personal to Political," *Buffalo News*, May 3, 1998.

47. Daphne Patai, *Heterophobia: Sexual Harassment and the Future of Feminism*, Rowman & Littlefield, 1998, p. 10.

48. Ibid., p. 13.

49. Ibid., p. 29.

50. Nancy Gibbs, "Cover Stories Behavior: When Is It Rape?," *Time*, June 3, 1991.

51. Patai, *Heterophobia*, p. 27.

52. Ibid., p. 34.

53. Ibid., p. 35.

54. Ibid., p. 49.

55. Ibid., p. 50.

56. Ibid., p. 57.

57. Richard McKenzie, "Adding Up the Cost of the Family-Leave Law," *Orange County Register,* January 31, 1993.

4 | IN THE CLASSROOM . . . BOYS WILL BE GIRLS

1. *Time,* June 17, 1996.

2. James Tooley, *The Miseducation of Women,* Ivan R. Dee, 2003, p. 37.

3. *New York Times,* March 30, 2002.

4. Ibid.

5. Peggy Orenstein, *Schoolgirls: Young Women, Self-Esteem, and the Confidence Gap,* Doubleday, 1994, p. 247.

6. Christina Hoff Sommers, "Capitol Hill's Girl Trouble; The Flawed Study Behind the Gender Equity Act," *Washington Post,* July 17, 1995.

7. *Congressional Record,* April 21, 1993, H1944.

8. *Congressional Record,* April 21, 1993, E998.

9. *Congressional Record,* September 15, 1993.

10. *Congressional Record,* April 21, 1993, H1953.

11. Christina Hoff Sommers, *The War Against Boys,* Simon & Schuster, 2000, p. 48.

12. Robert Lerner and Stanley Rothman, "Wonder Woman and the Wimp: Censorship of Textbooks by Liberal Feminists," *The Quill,* Vol. 78, No. 5, June 1990.

13. Robert Lerner and Stanley Rothman, "Newspeak, Feminist-Style," *Commentary,* April 1990.

14. Sommers, *The War Against Boys,* p. 51.

15. Christina Hoff Sommers, "A Feminist Camelot," *National Review,* September 2, 1996, p. 74.

16. Barbara Brotman, "Mystique and Memoir; In a New Book, Feminist

Betty Friedan Recalls the Bruises of Public and Private Battles," *Chicago Tribune*, May 31, 2000.

17. Sommers, *The War Against Boys*, p. 19.

18. Ibid., p. 24.

19. Ibid., pp. 36–37.

20. Rob Stein, "Boys, Girls Are Faring Equally, Study Finds," *Washington Post*, February 23, 2005.

21. Sandra Stotsky, "Why Johnny Won't Read," *Washington Post*, January 25, 2005, p. A15.

22. James Tooley, *The Miseducation of Women*, Ivan R. Dee, 2003, p. 192.

23. Ibid., p. 2.

24. Ibid., p. xiv.

25. Ibid., p. 94.

26. Ibid., pp. 117–118.

27. Ibid., p. 29.

28. Ibid., p. 210.

29. Ibid., p. 211.

30. Ibid., p. 208.

31. Ibid., p. 232.

32. Diana Furchtgott-Roth and Christine Stolba, *The Feminist Dilemma: When Success Is Not Enough*, AEI Press, 2001, pp. 24–25.

33. Ibid., pp. 29–30. (In 2001, women were awarded 44 percent of all doctorates.)

34. *Seattle Post-Intelligencer*, December 23, 2002.

35. Ibid.

36. Amy Hetzner, "As Girls Triumph in School, Some Worry About Boys," *Milwaukee Journal Sentinel*, July 1, 2001.

37. Furchtgott-Roth and Stolba, *The Feminist Dilemma*, pp. 27–28, 32.

38. Ibid., p. 34.

39. John Leo, "UMass Feminists Bash Academic Freedom," *U.S. News & World Report*, January 18, 1998.

40. Daphne Patai and Noretta Koertge, *Professing Feminism: Educational Indoctrination in Women's Studies*, Lexington Books, 2003, p. xiv.

41. NOW press release, January 20, 2005.

42. Heather Mac Donald, "Harvard's Diversity Grovel," *City Journal*, Manhattan Institute, June 2005.

43. Ibid.

44. Ibid.

45. *New York Times*, January, 23, 2005.

46. Kathryn Lopez, "Feminist Mythology," *National Review Online*, April 10, 2001.

47. Ibid.

48. IWF report, "Confession Without Guilt?," February 2001.

49. Judith Kleinfeld, "Truth to Power," *National Review Online*, January 25, 2005.

5 | SPOIL SPORTS—BOYS BENCHED

1. Christina Hoff Sommers, *Who Stole Feminism?: How Women Have Betrayed Women*, Simon & Schuster, 1995, pp. 15, 188–192.

2. Ibid., p. 192.

3. Furchtgott-Roth and Stolba, *The Feminist Dilemma*, p. 136.

4. Ibid.

5. *Washington Post*, April 22, 2004.

6. Jessica Gavora, *Tilting the Playing Field: Schools, Sports, Sex, and Title IX*, Encounter Books, 2002, p. 48.

7. Ibid., p. 158.

8. Kathryn Lopez, "A Fairer Game," *National Review Online*, April 6, 2005.

9. Kathy Kiely, "Surveys Can Be Used to Show Title IX Compliance," *USA Today*, March 22, 2005.

10. Kathryn Lopez, "Benched at Bowling Green," *National Review Online*, May 10, 2002.

11. Joseph H. Brown, "Augusta Greens Are Grass, Not Glass," *Tampa Tribune*, April 13, 2003.

12. *New York Times*, March 27, 2003.

13. *New York Times*, April 16, 2003.

14. Doug Ferguson, "One Year Later, the Road to the Masters Is About Golf," AP, March 11, 2004.

15. PR Newswire, April 7, 2005.

16. Kimberley Schuld, *Guide to Feminist Organizations*, Capital Research Center, 2002.

6 | G.I. JANES

1. Ann Scott Tyson, "The Expanding Role of GI Jane," *Christian Science Monitor*, March 3, 2003.

2. Rick Davis, "Despite Rule, U.S. Women on the Front Line in Iraq War," *USA Today*, June 27, 2005.

3. *USA Today*, September 7, 2004.

4. *San Antonio Express-News*, April 13, 2003.

5. *Chicago Tribune*, March 26, 2003.

6. *Washington Post*, March 26, 2003.

7. *Newsweek*, July 21, 2003.

8. *Women in Combat*, Report to the President, The Presidential Commission on the Assignment of Women in the Armed Forces, 1992.

9. Myriam Marquez, "Equal Rights Amendment Is the Right Thing to Do," *Orlando Sentinel*, April 6, 2003, p. G3.

10. *Chicago Tribune*, January 14, 1990.

11. Pamela Martineau and Steve Wiegand, "Fractured Families," *Sacramento Bee*, March 9, 2005.

12. Kirsten Schamberg, "Stresses of Battle Hit Female GIs Hard; VA Study Hopes to Find Treatment for Disorder," *Chicago Tribune*, March 20, 2005.

13. Ibid.

14. Pamela Martineau and Steve Wiegand, "Scarred Survivors," *Sacramento Bee*, March 8, 2005.

15. Michael Evans, "Women Pay Painful Price for Equal Military Training," *TimesOnline*, March 22, 2005.

16. *Washington Post,* November 23, 2003.

17. *Reader's Digest,* December 2004, p. 132.

18. *Detroit News,* July 11, 2004.

19. *Women in Combat,* Commission Report, 1992, p. 69.

20. Tom Bethell, "Our Meter Maid Military," *American Spectator,* July 1997.

21. *Crossfire,* CNN, April 23, 1993.

22. Ben Dobbin, "Women-Only Weekend Aims to Bolster Ranks of Female Firefighters," AP, November 27, 2004.

23. "The Burden of Saving Lives," *New York Times,* June 12, 2005.

7 | THE GENDER GAP DEBUNKED

1. "Abzug Presents Documents to Improve Women's Lives," *Washington Post,* October 27, 1977.

2. Gloria Steinem, *Outrageous Acts and Everyday Rebellions,* Henry Holt, 1995, p. 304.

3. "Abzug Presents Documents," *Washington Post,* October 27, 1977.

4. Donald T. Critchlow, *Phyllis Schlafly and Grassroots Conservatism: A Woman's Crusade,* Princeton University Press, 2005, p. 32.

5. "The Pedestal Has Crashed: Pride and Paranoia in Houston," *Washington Post,* November 23, 1977.

6. Ibid.

7. Ibid.

8. Ibid.

9. Ibid.

10. "The Sexual Balance of Power," *Washington Post,* March 4, 1984.

11. "Disagree over Importance of the Gender Gap," AP, December 9, 1983.

12. UPI, June 17, 1983.

13. UPI, August 26, 1983.

14. "A Woman's Political Place?" *Washington Post,* October 8, 1983.

15. Deborah Churchman, "Eleanor Smeal Talks About Women and Politics," *Christian Science Monitor,* March 20, 1984.

16. "Democrats Discuss Woman on the Ticket," *New York Times*, March 13, 1984.

17. Myra MacPherson, "Woman's Day; With Tears & Hope, Democratic Women Hail Their Heroine," *Washington Post*, July 20, 1984.

18. *Washington Post*, July 13, 1984.

19. "Women on Center Stage in Election," AP, October 5, 1984.

20. Ellen Goodman, "Yes, Ferraro Made a Difference," *Washington Post*, November 8, 1984.

21. Robin Morgan, ed., *Sisterhood Is Forever*, Washington Square Press, 2003, p. 32.

22. "Eleanor Smeal in Overdrive," *Washington Post*, November 24, 1985.

23. Michelle Malkin, "Hysterical Women for Kerry," *Jewish World Daily*, October 20, 2004.

24. *The News*, MSNBC, June 12, 2004.

25. "Did the Women's Vote Count?" *Chicago Sun-Times*, November 2004.

26. Marianne Means, "Symbolic Gestures and Tokenism Won't Close the Gender Gap," *Seattle Post-Intelligencer*, August 19, 1996.

27. Marianne Means, "Campaign's Silence Is Deafening," *Fort Worth Star-Telegram*, October 28, 1996.

28. Marianne Means, "President Still Has a Gender Gap," *Tulsa World*, March 29, 2002.

29. Marianne Means, "GOP Since Reagan Just Doesn't Get it," *Sun-Sentinel*, June 17, 2004.

30. "Gender Gap Myths and Legends," *Washington Times*, December 19, 2004.

31. *Today Show*, NBC, November 4, 2004.

32. "Planned Parenthood Chief Criticizes Kerry," AP, February 1, 2005.

33. Cal Thomas, "Democrats Try to Backtrack," *Washington Times*, December 29, 2004.

34. Karlyn Bowman, Independent Women's Forum Essay, November 15, 2004.

35. *Chicago Sun-Times*, February 28, 2004.

8| ABORTION—THE HOLY GRAIL

1. Kate Michelman, "Uphold It: Women Have the Right to Choose," *Charlotte Observer*, April 25, 2004.
2. Gloria Feldt, *The War on Choice*, Bantam Books, May 2004, p. 5.
3. Gloria Steinem, *Outrageous Acts and Everyday Rebellions*, Henry Holt, 1995, p. 165.
4. "Feminists for Life," *The American Feminist*, Summer 2001, p. 3.
5. "Feminist History," www.womendeservebetter.com.
6. Ibid.
7. Feminists for Life, *The American Feminist*, Spring 2004.
8. Ibid.
9. Ibid.
10. Erika Bachiochi, ed., *The Cost of "Choice": Women Evaluate the Impact of Abortion*, Encounter Books, 2004, p. 7.
11. Tom Hoppes, "Against the Grain: A Day in the Life of Serrin Foster," *Crisis*, June 2003.
12. David Tell, "Planned Un-Parenthood, *Roe* v. *Wade* at Thirty," *Weekly Standard*, January 27, 2003.
13. Feldt, *The War on Choice*, p. 45.
14. ABC News, "A Celebration: 100 Years of Great Women," April 30, 1999.
15. Maggie Gallagher, "Sanger; Public Persona Belies the Many Inadequacies of Activist's Personal Life," *Washington Times*, June 21, 1992.
16. Ibid.
17. New York University's Margaret Sanger Papers Project. The first volume in a projected four-volume series is *The Woman Rebel, 1900–1928*.
18. Tell, "Planned Un-Parenthood."
19. Jack Kenny, "Planned Parenthood Carries Out Founder's Vision," *New Hampshire Sunday News*, October 29, 2000.
20. Tell, "Planned Un-Parenthood."
21. Kenny, "Planned Parenthood."
22. Adam Nagourney, "Democrats Weigh De-emphasizing Abortion as an Issue," *New York Times*, December 24, 2004.

23. *Doe v. Bolton,* 410 U.S. at 193.

24. Schlafly, *Feminist Fantasies,* pp. 138–140.

25. Feldt, *The War on Choice,* p. 121.

26. "The Faye Wattleton Counterattack," *Washington Post,* October 14, 1987.

27. Ramesh Ponnuru, "Not Dead Yet," *National Review,* May 17, 1999.

28. "Surprise, Mom: I'm Anti-Abortion," *New York Times,* March 30, 2003.

29. "Activists Recruit New Generation for Abortion Fight," *Atlanta Journal-Constitution,* April 24, 2004.

30. Ibid.

31. Feldt, *The War on Choice,* p. 25.

32. Ellen Goodman, "Pro-Choice Women Look to the Wobbly Middle," *Chicago Tribune,* April 16, 1989.

33. Michelman, "Uphold It," April 25, 2004.

34. Feldt, *The War on Choice,* p. 228.

35. Ponnuru, "Not Dead Yet."

36. Kristin Day, "A Pro-Choice Party No More," *National Review Online,* December 2, 2004.

37. Robert P. Casey, "The Gag Rule Party," *Wall Street Journal,* August 23, 1996.

38. *The Hotline,* March 11, 2005.

39. *The Hotline,* March 14, 2004.

40. Rod Dreher, "The Cost of Choice, Choosing Life," *National Review,* April 8, 2002, p. 36.

41. Nat Hentoff, "There Are Many Votes Kerry Won't Get Due to Abortion," *Morning Call,* Allentown, PA, September 22, 2004.

42. David Stout, "An Abortion Rights Advocate Says He Lied About Procedure," *New York Times,* February 26, 1997.

43. www.nrlc.org/abortion/pba/roevwademyths.html.

44. *Crossfire,* CNN, April 2, 1996.

45. Kate Michelman, "Women's Rights Mandates Vote for Kerry," *Seattle Post-Intelligencer,* October 29, 2004.

46. Feldt, *The War on Choice,* p. 17.

47. Feldt, *The War on Choice,* Introduction by Sally Blackmun, p. xix.

48. Ellen Goodman, "March Marks Passing of Baton Between Generations," *Contra Costa Times*, April 27, 2004.
49. Bachiochi, *The Cost of "Choice,"* p. 55.
50. Ibid., p. 54.

CONCLUSION | MOTHER NATURE IS A BITCH

1. *New York Times*, January 18, 2005; Stuart Taylor, "Why Feminist Careerists Neutered Larry Summers," *NationalJournal.com*, February 7, 2005.
2. Simon Baron-Cohen, *The Essential Difference*, Basic Books, 2003, p. 10.
3. Dianne Hales, *Just Like a Woman*, Bantam Books, 1999, p. 4.
4. Christina Hoff Sommers, *Who Stole Feminism*, Simon and Schuster, quoting Ann Ferguson, University of Massachusetts Press, 1994, p. 265.
5. Daphne Patai and Noretta Koertge, *Professing Feminism*, Lexington Books, 2003, p. 318.
6. ABC News Special, Transcript #57, February 1, 1995.
7. Hales, *Just Like a Woman*, quoting Raquel Gur of the University of Pennsylvania, p. 242.
8. Jon Sall, "Gender Debate Flares Anew," *Chicago Sun-Times*, March 17, 1996.
9. Ibid.
10. Katie Mulvaney, "25 Years Later, Women's Studies Still Opens Eyes," *Providence Journal*, May 8, 2005.
11. Sall, "Gender Debate Flares Anew."
12. Hales, *Just Like a Woman*, p. 121.
13. Robert Pool, *Eve's Rib*, Crown, 1994.
14. Steven E. Rhoads, *Taking Sex Differences Seriously*, Encounter Books, 2004, p. 26.
15. Matt Ridley, *The Red Queen, Sex, and the Evolution of Human Nature*, Harper Perennial, 2003, pp. 249–250.
16. Ibid., p. 248.
17. Ibid., p. 178.

18. Ibid., p. 180.

19. Maureen Dowd, "Men Just Want Mommy," *New York Times*, January 13, 2005, p. 35.

20. George Gilder, *Men and Marriage*, Pelican, 1986.

21. Rhoads, *Taking Sex Differences Seriously*, p. 49.

22. Hales, *Just Like a Woman*, p. 29.

23. Rhoads, *Taking Sex Differences Seriously*, p. 5.

24. Ibid., pp. 96–97.

25. Carrie L. Lukas, "Sex (Ms.) Education," *Independent Women's Forum*, February 10, 2005, p. 7.

26. Leonard Sax, M.D., Ph.D., *Why Gender Matters: What Parents and Teachers Need to Know About the Emerging Science of Sex Differences*, Doubleday, 2005, p. 128.

27. Mary Eberstadt, *Home-Alone America*, Sentinel, 2004, p. 125.

28. Lukas, "Sex (Ms.) Education," p. 9.

29. Peggy Burch, "Assembling a Fractured Youth; Writing Her Truth Sets Walker Free," *Commercial Appeal*, Memphis, January 18, 2002.

30. Amy Doolittle, *Washington Times*, March 15, 2005.

31. Sax, *Why Gender Matters*, p. 118.

32. Rhoads, *Taking Sex Differences Seriously*, p. 98.

33. Hales, *Just Like a Woman*, p. 313.

34. Ibid.

35. Ridley, *The Red Queen*, p. 218.

36. Deborah Soloman, "Reimagining Boyhood," *New York Times*, June 13, 2004.

37. Baron-Cohen, *The Essential Difference*, pp. 52, 55, 83.

38. Ibid., p. 129.

39. Rhoads, *Taking Sex Differences Seriously*, pp. 203–221.

40. Baron-Cohen, *The Essential Difference*, pp. 57–59.

41. Ridley, *The Red Queen*, p. 256.

42. Rhoads, *Taking Sex Differences Seriously*, p. 145.

43. Baron-Cohen, *The Essential Difference*, p. 36.

44. Ibid., pp. 42–44.

45. Ibid., pp. 8–9.

46. Roger Kimball, "Where Is Hercules When You Need Him?" *The New Criterion's* weblog, Armavirumque, www.newcriterion.com/weblog/armavirumque.html, June 3, 2005.

47. Hales, *Just Like a Woman*, 241.

48. Ibid., p. 65.

49. Ibid., p. 66.

50. Ibid., p. 64.

51. Ibid., p. 241.

52. Ibid., p. 67.

53. Ibid., p. 244.

54. Rhoads, *Taking Sex Differences Seriously*, pp. 27–28.

55. Sax, *Why Gender Matters*, p. 25.

56. Ridley, *The Red Queen*, pp. 250–251.

57. Ibid., pp. 254–255.

58. Baron-Cohen, *The Essential Difference*, pp. 102–103.

59. Rhoads, *Taking Sex Differences Seriously*, p. 29.

60. Ibid.

61. Ibid., p. 31.

62. Ibid., p. 248.

63. Baron-Cohen, *The Essential Difference*, p. 70.

64. Ibid., p. 185.

65. Sax, *Why Gender Matters*, p. 93.

66. Ibid., p. 99.

67. Ibid., p. 106.

68. Ibid., p. 107.

69. Ibid., p. 112.

70. Michael Dobbs, "U.S. Plans to Relax Restrictions on Single-Sex Schools," *Washington Post*, March 4, 2004.

71. Teresa Mendez, "Separating the Sexes: A New Direction for Public Education?" *Christian Science Monitor*, May 25, 2004; Massie Ritsch, "Single-Gender Schools Gaining Favor, Success; Education: Some Pupils Like Segregated Classrooms, but Critics Say It's Not the Real World," *Los Angeles Times*, May 28, 2002.

72. Rhoads, *Taking Sex Differences Seriously*, p. 162.

73. Ibid.
74. Ibid., p. 163.
75. Ibid., p. 168.
76. Baron-Cohen, *The Essential Difference*, p. 81.
77. Rhoads, *Taking Sex Differences Seriously*, p. 184.
78. Baron-Cohen, *The Essential Difference*, pp. 92, 76.
79. Ibid., p. 131.

Index